D0108359

FIND YOUR CALLING, LOVE YOUR LIFE

Paths to Your Truest Self
in Life and Work

Martha Finney
and
Deborah Dasch

SIMON & SCHUSTER

Simon & Schuster
Rockefeller Center
1230 Avenue of the Americas
New York, NY 10020

Simon & Schuster and colophon are registered trademarks
of Simon & Schuster Inc.

Designed by Jeanette Olender
Manufactured in the United States of America

1   3   5   7   9   10   8   6   4   2

Library of Congress Cataloging-in-Publication Data
Finney, Martha I.
Find your calling, love your life : paths to your truest self in life and
work / Martha Finney, Deborah Dasch.
p. cm.
1. Vocational guidance.   2. Vocation.   I. Dasch, Deborah A.
HF5381.F478   1998
331.7'02—dc21   97-36443   CIP
ISBN 0-684-83169-4

For Marjorie L. Bank, undersea journalist,
fine art photographer, and dear friend

We dedicate this book to the memory of Marjorie Bank, whose life's work embodied the very essence of finding and living a calling. Marjorie's knowledge of marine biology and animal behavior, combined with her outrageous sense of humor, made her one of the most beloved speakers in the scuba world. Nothing gave Marjorie greater joy than sharing with others what she experienced under the surface. And it was her conviction that she was fulfilling her purpose on this planet that brought a magical quality to her lectures on marine life.

When we started talking about writing this book, Marjorie was the first person we thought of who was actually living her calling. The pain we feel over her untimely death also reminds us that we all have a finite time on this earth to discover that which ignites our passions and inspires us to follow *our* true calling.

Acknowledgments

While interviewing the individuals profiled in this book, we heard again and again about the angels in their lives who had a hand in helping them realize their calling. We too have been blessed with angelic guidance during the course of writing this book. Beginning with our literary agent, Denise Stinson, who saw what we saw from the very start. We are indebted to Mary Ann Naples and Laurie Chittenden of Simon & Schuster for their incisive editorial instincts, good sense, and faith in us. We are grateful that they took our book under their wing.

We thank our friends and colleagues who contributed valuable insights, particularly Peter Sylvan, who was an early supporter and idea-generator. We especially want to thank Nancy Noll, who unwittingly triggered the idea for *Find Your Calling, Love Your Life* when she sent us Marianne Williamson's book, *A Return to Love,* as a Christmas present in 1992.

Martha has a few thanks of her own. To Lenore Horowitz, Hank Altman, and John Adams: thank you for bringing me here. To Carol Dayton and Jennifer Deitz: thank you for keeping the Fancy Feast flowing while I was away. And to Deb, Kathy, Lil, Nancy, and Laura for the calling of friendship. Dad, thanks for teaching me to imagine what there might be. Rick, thanks for Central Park and the American Café, the makings of our first great stories.

On a personal note, Deborah wishes to thank Donna Stephens, for her keen insights into the spiritual connection between work and joy and the gentle reminder that God's grace is there for all of us. To Sheran Hartwell: thank you for our friendship, which began in your office the day you hired me. And to my parents, whose love and support has both inspired and nourished me on my own life's journey.

Finally, we want to thank all the people who spent hours with us and our tape recorders for this book. We're grateful for their willingness to talk so candidly about the meaning of work in their lives. Oliver Wendell Holmes once said, "Every calling is great when greatly pursued." We can think of no truer description of each of the individuals within these pages and of no better words to aspire to in our own working lives.

Contents

CONTENTS

Introduction

Greatness Is Your Birthright

*I think most of us are looking for a
calling, not a job. Most of us . . . have jobs that
are too small for our spirit.*

NORA WATSON
editor, in *Working*, by Studs Terkel

"How did you two meet?"

Who among us hasn't been tempted to ask that question
when we encounter a couple so obviously well suited for
each other? We all know the signs of a match made in
heaven (or at least we like to think we do): shared interests
and goals, a mutually passionate reveling in each other's
company, a greatness—a fire—that each is able to achieve
as an individual because of the influence and inspiration of
the other, the ability to go through the hard times with rel-

ative ease because of their shared vision of their lives as a whole.

For what's a great love but the exhilarating chance to connect to the outside world in a new way, and a reintroduction to ourselves as glowing, happy individuals packed with energy and joy and new purpose?

Those are the same feelings you can expect from your work.

Just as we've been taught that we are destined for that joy through the love of another person, we've also been taught that we are destined for the same kind of love match through our work: bright and shining careers that will help save the world in some way, once we discover and cultivate our innate talents.

Like true love, true work promises us immortality. It places us among the heroes, shining with a beauty of mythic proportions.

As children we were imprinted with the belief that our true life's work will help us meet each day with profound joy and pride, an effectiveness that makes us stand tall in our shoes. *Each of us, we were taught, will move through life on a trail blazed uniquely for us, paved with the magic dust of good fortune, and lined with doors that would automatically open at our slightest knock.*

And through the graceful efforts of our natural talents and the relaxed, energized, easy passion we bring to exercising our unique gifts, we will leave the world a better place than it was when we arrived.

We have moved through our years with a haunting hunger for true love and true work. But each passing day of our childhood and adolescence has taken us further and further away from the faith that greatness is out there waiting for us to claim it as our birthright.

Disenchanted teachers, report cards, discouraging career counselors, job application forms, one-sheet résumés, uninspired supervisors, the headlines—all seem to conspire against our personal faith and vision of the heroic journey we are supposed to be on. Somewhere along the way we gave up our heroic mission and settled for survival.

And so we wait for something to happen. Some bolt out of the sky. A heavenly visitation. A vivid dream. The coincidence of a life-changing invitation that comes within an hour of getting fired. Something unmistakable; something undeniable. Something unignorable. Something easy.

That something never seems to come.

But every now and then we get a glimmering of what can be. We run across a heavenly match. When it's a love match, we just can't help but ask, "How did you two meet?"

And when we meet people who are obviously in touch with their true life's work, we ask, "How did you get that job?"

We don't ask those questions because we expect to be able to discover the same joy exactly the same way they did. We know better than to expect to find our own true love by standing in the same theater line, going to the same gas station on a lucky day, or balancing a plastic champagne glass at the very next museum reception.

Likewise, just because our friend has found unparalleled joy from, say, collecting geological samples from live volcanoes, we're not about to show up at the personnel office with résumé in hand, expecting to share in the thrill of volcanic ash.

But to hear their stories is, in effect, to touch the hem of their garment. Perhaps a blessing will rub off on us. And we will magically awaken, be transformed, and finally come into our own as a person with work to do on this earth.

Then we will be able to hear our own calling.

You're Already on the Right Path

There is a calling with your name on it. And you're already answering it. You have a unique personality, combined with a one-of-a-kind set of skills, talents, passions, and experiences. All of these have combined and conspired to put you on the road to your true life's work—work that you can do like no one else on this planet.

When you marry skills, passions, and experiences, you produce a life for yourself that is larger, easier, and more effective than you could have dreamed of in all your years struggling in mismatched jobs. You blossom and courageously explore psychological, emotional, and occupational frontiers that before seemed so far out of reach. You have come into your own in every aspect of your life, not just the side of you that brings home the paycheck.

How does it feel to find your true work? The same way it feels to find your true love! It is one of those cosmic *Aha*s that tell you: At last! This is what I'm alive for! This is why I was born! This is why I breathe!

In our research, we discovered that callings come in many forms and job titles. We've also come to the conclusion that sometimes it is not so much what you do, but the way your work reaches down and touches that limitless well of passion within you.

Your calling might lead you to a glamorous job. Or it can help you look at the work you've been doing all along in a brand-new light. You may even have more than one calling in your life, as your experiences and skills move you through your years.

The tricky part, we find, is keeping the faith and a look-out for that sublime satisfaction that comes from finding and doing your life's work. It's hard to do in the face of so many messages in society that work is drudgery. Yes, as Nora Watson said, jobs are too small for people. But the potential for joy, satisfaction, and growth in doing your life's work is boundless!

So to counteract all of society's messages that work is a ruinous waste of precious hours, we decided to dedicate our own talents to interviewing people who have found their true life's work.

Find Your Calling, Love Your Life was written to give you the chance to spend some time in the company of individuals who have found personal greatness and growth through their work.

When we began our research, we thought that each chapter would be a description of our subjects' work, what they do, and how they feel about it. But as our conversations continued, we discovered that each profile had some-thing to say about an *aspect* of finding one's calling: the patience, the faith, the drive, the need to keep your ear tuned to the melody that sings only to you.

Each calling is unique. In fact you probably have several different callings—one right after the other or all at once. And each path toward each calling may be very different.

No one can give you a step-by-step program for finding your true life's work. The best we can do is teach you—and teach ourselves, for that matter—by the examples we've found around the country.

The lessons you need are within these pages. Maybe it's a career idea you were looking for. Maybe it's a wisdom that will rise from the pages and touch your heart unexpectedly. Maybe it's patience. Maybe it's perspective. Or maybe it's the happy reassurance that you have so many companions on this road of searching out meaningful ways of spending your days. Our hope is that the words of the people within these pages will give you the faith you will need when the way isn't quite so clear.

No matter what their callings may be, all of our subjects share the dignity of expressing themselves in their true life's work. And that dignity is portable. No matter what their jobs may be—no matter who signs their paychecks—they know who their ultimate employer is. Some call that employer God. Some call it passion. Some call it simply the right thing to do.

But no matter what you call it, it's enough to know that that's where your deepest security resides. Find your calling, and you will never be out of work. There will always be something to do.

Part One

WHEN THE
CALL COMES

Social myth would have us believe that the ones
among us who are called are the lucky few who
discovered as children that wonderful thing they excel
at with a natural ease. But you don't have to be a
child prodigy to hear the call. Your call will come to
you anytime, anywhere, any way.

The way your calling will reveal itself to you will be
as unique as the calling itself. Perhaps you will notice
it by what you're doing. Or by what you're not
doing. Or where you are. Or where you aren't.

Or a mysterious drive to learn something new, just
when you thought it was time to retire.

The good news is that when you're ready to hear the
call, you will. How you answer will be up to you.

1

Trust Your Basic Nature

*I was able to resurrect myself here. It was a rush
so powerful, it scared me. I've become part of the town,
and the town has become part of me. I've finally been
able to be me, and not only am I appreciated,
I'm actually sought after.*

TODD GARRETT

28, Manager, Café

Probably the most challenging career we can have is the tough job of being ourselves. The value of our calling is that it requires us to express the most fundamental truths of who we are. Our true life's work returns us to ourselves.

Self-recognition and self-acceptance may be our calling's first gifts to ourselves. And to the world. Because only then can the serious work get done.

But it's hard for us to accept ourselves for who we are.

When our calling presents itself, we often reject it or put it off. Our muddled perspective delays our destiny: The timing is wrong. Or we don't think we're up to the task yet. Or we want to get something else done first. Or we'll do it once we're rich. Or we'll do it once we're happy. But your calling wants you just the way you are.

Sooner or later your calling will speak louder than your doubts. And then you will be amazed at how easy it really is to be you.

Visit the popular downtown café where Todd Garrett works, and you'll find a café completely different from today's trendy spots where people sip and posture in chic anonymity. This is a gathering place of young mothers with strollers, day laborers dressed for the weather, college professors and students, one ninety-four-year-old military retiree who comes in twice a week for a sociable cup or two, and even the town's eccentrics, who will be treated with respect and called by name.

Todd Garrett, officially the café's manager, is unofficially the café's mayor. Come once and you'll get a great cup of coffee. Come twice and he'll greet you by name. Come four or five times and your drink will be waiting for you by the time the long line ushers you up to the cash register. Todd has spotted you in the crowd already, and your coffee will be poured just the way you like it.

Todd will tell you that he's in the food and beverage profession— the service industry. But his calling is to make people feel good.

Todd is tall, his smiling face usually clearing the heads of the younger college kids who work there part-time. And Todd is nice. There is a good word to say to everyone. And Todd is resourceful. He knows the person you need to call to get done what you need to get done.

And Todd has come a long way. His first calling was the long journey back to himself. Although only twenty-eight, he's already lived a lifetime of resisting his basic nature, only to return to it once again. And to find a community that has been waiting just for him.

I never intended to go into the food service industry. I just fell into it. I was in college for a couple of years, majoring in physics and then fine arts. But then because of a lot of family issues, I left home and took a job as a waiter in a nearby restaurant.

I'll never forget that first afternoon. Something just clicked into place for me.

I was thrown to the tigers that day. I had never been a waiter before, and that first afternoon I had a whole section of thirteen tables to manage alone. It was lunchtime. It got insane. But I handled it. I worked it. Here were people who needed me. They wanted their lunch, and my job was to get it to them within their lunch hour.

That restaurant was it for me. I needed a place away from my family problems, and the restaurant pulled me in and embraced me. And I let it embrace me. It gave me a place where I could belong. I was introduced to worlds I had never known before: I was serving young professionals, parents of the college kids, and the blue-collar workers who made manhole covers at a factory in a different part of town.

That's where I discovered I could soak in lots of information, including people's names. Say you're presented with a pressure situation. It's Friday happy hour, the place is packed, everyone wants their drinks and meals yesterday. So much data is coming at you. This person wants their steak rare. Another likes their steak medium. More gin than tonic here. More tonic than gin there. Olives, not lime. Lime, not olives.

I only had two ways to go. I could let that pressure break me. Or I could just absorb all the information and use it to my advantage. And that's what I did.

Over the next three years Todd's talents served him well. He became the youngest manager of the restaurant chain. And at twenty-one he was the youngest legal bartender in the most popular bar in town. With pockets full of cash, and night-owl hours, he had popularity, he had power. But soon he had to stop.

One of the reasons I did so well was because I was also one of the nicest guys in the business. I was never a bad person, but I was bad to myself. I lived upstairs from the bar, so I could roll out of bed into the bar. And then roll out of the bar into bed when the sun was coming up. There was alcohol and there were drugs, all the things that go with a fast life. I had access to anything I wanted in that town.

There were car accidents. I don't know why I was behind the wheel at those times. But I remember the times standing on the side of the road with the police officer. But I never got charged with anything and I have no record. This was a small town and everyone knew each other. So I just got warned and taken home.

You know the expression, "Work hard and play hard"? Well, in that business, you work hard and you play awfully hard.

After a while the fast lifestyle wore me out. I finally reached the point where I needed a break. I was spending money as fast as I could make it. I was tired and I was thin. And I was only twenty-three at the time, so you can imagine the pace I was at. It just got to the point where reality grabbed ahold of my sensibility. If there was any one thing that changed my life, I would say it was time.

I didn't have a near-death experience or cause someone else to have a near-death experience. But something just clicked. I realized that I was on a downward spiral. And I just had to stop.

All my past experience is responsible for who I am today. This time of my life was a negative experience, but that in itself was a benefit. It showed me what not to be.

Maybe it was reality. Maybe it was because he was tired and thin. And maybe it was because he was a new husband, with a new bride and a new baby on the way. Maybe all of these changes conspired to convince him that he needed to quit the fast life and become a family man with family-man hours. One afternoon he spotted a daytime-television ad for auto mechanics school, and he took his first step away from himself. Away from people. And a painful, lonely era would begin for him, working with things and with people who just didn't get him.

The automotive career was really a whim, a curiosity that offered me the possibility of a healthier lifestyle. So after the training, I worked for a couple of garages in town.

I had never been lonelier and more stressed out. It was just me and the car. I was working with cars and inanimate objects. I'm generalizing here, but auto mechanics are typically drawn to their field because they are more comfort-

able with engines than with people. Their technical training does not provide much room for philosophy. They're
introverted, and I'm an extrovert with a strong, childlike,
playful nature.

I wanted to talk to the other mechanics, but they didn't
want to talk back. They would just look at me and say,
"Oh, that's just crazy Todd," or "Silly Todd," or "Todd being Todd." But what good is it to be Todd when it's lost in
a huge garage?

No cars blew up on me or anything, and I was some-
what successful. But I could never be myself. I lost myself. I
was stagnating, my brain was bored, my ability to express
my energy was being dissipated.

But I was trying to change myself to fit my idea of what
a conventional family man is, working 8 to 5. But I needed
people, I needed to experience people. And I wasn't bringing my true self either to my work or to my family.

*Thinking it was the restaurant business he missed, Todd left his
automotive career to open a new restaurant with a friend from the old
days. But the road back to himself was still far away.*

This new business was a chance to get back into food. It
was the chance to work with a friend, to get back into familiar work, and to maybe make more money. This was a
ground-floor prospect. If it worked, we were going to be
rich. If it didn't work, we were going to be poor.

I really hoped things would be better, but soon I was working insane hours, commuting forty-five minutes each way to our business, which wasn't really a full-service restaurant but more of a take-out place. We served really delicious southern barbecue, but we were in an economically defunct area. And we just didn't have the traffic we were expecting.

We did everything we could to make this business fly, but we could only do so much. We did very, very low numbers, but we mostly just sat there until 9:00 P.M. watching a little television. I was just dead inside.

I was making such an effort to change myself for the sake of my family. But the reality was that my marriage was doomed from the start. It was such a short time from the time we met to the engagement to the marriage. And three weeks later we were pregnant with Sam.

In society, when we get married and have a family we're programmed to dissolve the delineations of who we are for the sake of the larger unit. The marriage I chose showed me that I needed to not dissolve that delineation of who I am. The whole turn of events, as quick as they are, showed me that indeed I didn't know who I was—through the marriage I gained more of an understanding of who I am by the wrong choices I made.

Looking back on it now, it's clear that I've spent my

twenties learning about who I am by discovering all the things I'm not. It's been a process of exploration, and that exploration has involved big life decisions and big life occurrences. It was the *lack* of love, of passion, of even friendship in my marriage, that made me realize what I wanted from myself and from a family life.

In retrospect I know that Sam was the reason why we were brought together. He is such a blessing to this world, such a dynamic little boy who makes so many people so happy. And he was not going to come from any other combination but his mother and me. And the few hours of consciousness that I had every day between sleep and work was the time I wanted to spend loving my son.

In the middle of his misery a friend of his wife's heard that the local café needed a new manager. The four owners were breaking away from a partnership that wasn't working, and they discovered that they needed an experienced food-service manager. And fast. Todd's special way with people and experience as a quick-thinking manager made him the perfect candidate for the job.

It happened with one phone call. It was one of those things that was so right. It was easy because it was so right.

We all came together and bonded. They needed me and I needed them. The café was only six months old, and from the get-go they gave me control. And the focus for all of us was the café and what it would mean to the town and our customers. We were all on the same wavelength of what our focus was going to be.

I enjoy what we've created. And I've been involved in almost every step. We have an atmosphere here that welcomes so many different people, so many ranges of characters and personalities.

I was able to resurrect myself here. It was a rush so powerful it scared me. I've become part of the town, and the town has become part of me. I've finally been able to be me, and not only am I appreciated, I'm actually sought after.

Part of my initial training in what it means to run a first-rate café was a trip to an international coffee and tea trade show in Austria within a couple of months of starting work. There I was in Vienna going to seminars and the trade show. I had never been out of the country, and there I was socializing and interacting with people from all over the world.

Only a year before, I had been an unhappy mechanic.

Isn't it amazing the way life works? I appreciate every bit and every detail of how it unfolds in so many unexpected ways. Each life's event is a tool for introducing yourself to yourself. No single event or decision was the catalyst to change my life. I just grew as I went along. Isn't that the way it is with most people?

I do believe that things are predetermined. I believe that everybody's put here for a reason. I've developed such a life in such a short period of time. I now have a great relationship with my ex-wife; we work together very well to raise a fabulous son. I've gone from a self-destructive job and social life to a terrible loneliness to finally work that allows me to combine the best of my outgoing nature with healthy hours and a sane lifestyle.

The way this café is run and what it means to the people who work there and the customers who come here reflect a lot of what I bring to it as a happy, healthy person. I bring to the café the best of who I am every day. And I'm recognized and appreciated for that. Whenever I get caught up in things, I have to remind myself that I'm not even thirty yet. I'm glad all this happened when I was young.

I'm glad I didn't wait until I was fifty and realize that the last thirty years I had been untrue to myself. Not that it would be too late to start something new, but how awful it would be to see that there were thirty years of blocked-off time when I could have contributed something.

But for me it's less a verbal recognition than a personal feeling of being at ease with life. Things click into place when you're doing what you're meant to do.

I'm here to make people feel good.

2

Follow Those Twists
of Fate

*We don't know what we don't know. There's a whole
world of possibilities out there. And just to be able to say,
"I don't know about this," is a huge step to finding
out what those possibilities are.*

MYRA DOMS

49, Outplacement Counselor

When we wake up in the morning, none of us ever really
know how the day will play itself out. Maybe before sunset
our lives will have been changed in an instant. A chance
meeting. An unexpected job offer. An abrupt dismissal. Or
perhaps we're confronted with a choice that challenges our
most preciously held beliefs.

We know intellectually that to choose job security
over our values is a bad trade. We all know that job se-

curity is a rapidly disappearing illusion. But would we have the strength to make the right choice when we must weigh our morals against our mortgage?

The next time your life presents you with a crossroads, turn toward your heart. It may be scary. It may be uncertain.

Then again, it just may be that simple twist of fate that will put you on the road to your calling.

Hardly anyone is happy with the circumstances that bring them to Myra Doms's sunny, contemporary Sacramento office. Most people who seek Myra's help are there because they have just joined the three million Americans who have been downsized, reengineered out of their position, or just plain fired.

Myra is an outplacement counselor retained by their former employers to help them step into the next chapter of their lives. Her job, they think, is to help them find a new job.

Her role, she knows, is to help them find themselves first. Only then, she says, will they find the careers that have been waiting for them all along.

Myra is sleek and chic; only her raspy voice gives a hint of her hard-smoking years working in corporate human resources, facing difficult choices that ultimately pitted her family's security and mate-

rial comforts against her ethics. The choice she finally made brought her to this prestigious international outplacement firm—as a client herself. And because of that simple twist of fate, she can work with her clients—or, as she calls them, candidates—and be able to say every step of the way, "I understand, I've been there too."

Each candidate who passes through Myra's reception area must do what she did the first time she visited the office as a candidate herself: come to terms with the gigantic brandy snifter stuffed with champagne corks. Each cork represents a bottle that was opened to celebrate another success story. And the cork bears the name of the former candidate who was transformed into a "graduate."

So many corks, so many successfully placed candidates, and each new candidate is afraid to be the one to break a winning streak.

Usually people are very frightened because they don't know what outplacement is. Their company has terminated them, and now they're going to a stranger at a company they have never heard of, and they believe their fate is in this person's hands.

I usually say in the first meeting with a candidate that most people will say to themselves, "I'm the sole exception to this process. I'm the only one this isn't going to work for."

We take people where they are in their lives, try to open them up to possibilities and inspire them to believe they can get another job. Each graduate who has a cork in that snifter started out believing he wasn't going to succeed, either.

My job is to help my candidates empower themselves and start realizing how many choices they really do have. It's not unusual for the candidates to end up with three or four offers. As they gain confidence in their ability to find a job (not just any job—that's slam-dunk, you can do that tomorrow—but the job that is right in their personal and professional growth), as soon as they begin to recognize that they have personal value, they become different people.

Many people feel it's a life-changing process. I've had candidates say to me, "I didn't know it's about life planning. I thought it was just about career planning."

And I'd say back, "We never tell you that or you'd go away!"

The events that brought Myra to this firm were a series of life-changing decisions and choices she herself agonized over. Once a human resources executive bringing home a six-figure salary, Myra eventually found herself helping the newly acquired company transform itself into a new entity—one she didn't like and one that was run by individuals who began demanding from her actions that she describes as unethical, immoral, and illegal.

I was the senior vice president of human resources and corporate services for a $2 billion company, which got acquired and was relocating to another state. I ended up resigning because they asked me to do things I just couldn't do. They said, "Are you or are you not a senior vice president of this company?" And I answered, "What time is it? Because I have a feeling I'm not going to be one for very long."

I won't wear stripes for anybody. So I resigned. I was terrified. I alternated between feeling on top of the world and sobbing. I had never been without a job before, and I had never before had a job that paid that well. But I was worn out emotionally from working so hard at being something I wasn't.

During the time that led up to this moment, I was taking full responsibility for it not working out. I figured I'm doing something terribly wrong. It didn't occur to me that they might be crooks and that they might be wacko.

So Myra, for fifteen years a highly compensated professional who hired people, was suddenly in the job market herself. And thus began a search for herself as much as a search for a new position. This was a harder task than she expected. But she wasn't alone in the process—her outplacement counselor guided her at every step.

I had never had to look for a job before because I had always been recruited. I knew how to hire people, but I had never been on the other side. And I didn't handle it very well. I got interviews for jobs that I should have wanted, but I'd always self-destruct during the interview. It was like having an out-of-body experience where I could watch myself put a gun to my head and say something that would get me eliminated. Every fiber in my being was screaming, "You don't want this anymore!"

My counselor said, "There's something wrong with this picture. Why are you doing this?"

I realized I didn't want to do this kind of work anymore. I didn't want to play on the political battlefield anymore. I didn't want to travel 80 percent of my time anymore. I discovered that there isn't enough money if you can't sleep at night, and there really isn't enough money if you can't look at yourself in the mirror. I didn't like looking in the mirror.

If that meant living in a tent, then I was prepared to start looking for a tent.

Everyone doing outplacement counseling needs to go through a time of terror when they are unemployed and think they aren't going to make it. Then you can come in and say to your candidates, "I know what it feels like to re-cycle cans to pay the rent and to think you'll never get a job you liked as well as the one you lost."

Myra's calling and destiny were right under her nose. And every-one closest to her could see it, but she continued to resist—not know-

ing what outplacement counseling really was, even though she was herself a candidate. But another twist of fate stepped in and she found herself thrown into her true life's work. Anyway.

My counselor told me she wanted me talk to people who knew me really well from way back and ask them, "If you were me, what would you be doing?" It's important, she told me, to go back as early in life as possible, because it is the people who knew you when you were really young who might have the truest picture of what really motivates you.

So I did, and at least eight people told me I should go into outplacement counseling myself! My response? "Oh, I don't want to work with unemployed people!"

This is not working with unemployed people, it's working with people in transition. I know that sounds trendy, but it's true. It's working with people leaving something and going through a very chaotic time and having a new beginning. And every person can do that, not just highly paid executives.

So I resisted until one day my counselor said that a workshop leader had just gotten into a car accident, and since I had training experience, would I mind taking over the first class? And here I am.

While each candidate's passage to his or her next career chapter is unique, Myra puts her candidates through an elaborate battery of sophisticated psychological and aptitude tests. In the process she leads them to new conclusions about themselves and what it means to build a working life today. The first step is to reassure them that being laid off does not necessarily mean they're failures.

They believe their careers are dead. That they've finally been Peter Principled, that people have found out that they're not as good as they thought—that impostor syndrome. No matter how you color a layoff, an individual is going to say, "Why me?"

The fact is, it's no-fault divorce in the employment market today. The current statistics show that we'll have seven to eight jobs in our lifetime and three of those we will leave involuntarily.

We have to get good at seeing what the possibilities are, because there is no such thing as lifetime employment and there never was.

The whole nature of work is being changed. It's not necessarily negative, you just have to find your new place. If you don't do that until you have to, things are going to get a lot harder. If we're being aware of our happiness and what we should be doing, it should be better every time we move. It shouldn't be a disaster. It should be an improvement.

What's important is to realize that the world is full of opportunities that we don't know about yet. And a rewarding part of the adventure is opening up to new ideas. We don't know what we don't know. There's a whole world of possibilities out there. And just to be able to say, "I don't know about this," is a huge step to finding out what those possibilities are.

Myra left her former employer out of what she calls major philosophical differences and entered a brand-new career with a new evolving philosophy of career development and how it drives growth in all aspects of life.

We really are a work in progress. I have so many people say to me I would really like your job. But I tell them what they really want is to feel about their work the way I do. That's doable for everybody—if they're willing to take the time or there is sufficient pain in their present situation.

Money is not a satisfier long-term, but short-term it certainly can be. But if you ask what people really want, you'll hear they want peace of mind and the feeling that what they are doing has value. Of course, peace of mind has a huge financial component to it. If you're not meeting your basic needs financially, you're not going to have peace of mind.

Each individual has to define what success means. But it comes down to knowing that you fit and that who you are naturally is exactly what your company needs. It feels so good when you're working with someone who wants you, the way you do things and the value you bring to your company.

You're not trying to change things to fit into someone else's box. You are presenting yourself to the company and saying, "Here's what I am, here's what I do, and here's what I bring. Is this something you have a need for?"

The job search should be going out and finding a need in the marketplace. And nothing feels better than finding the need that you can genuinely fill.

Finding our calling is a journey. We may not know where it is right away. We don't know what it looks like. We can't even say when we'll get there. We just know it's there so deep in our hearts that when it does come out it's genuine and unmistakable.

3

Stay Flexible
and Open

You have to constantly give to others to
make more room inside.

LEROY "THE HERBMAN" WILTON

57, Organic Herb Gardener

Keeping your eyes open to what's possible and being willing to adjust your focus will help you locate your life's genuine purpose. And perhaps, if need be, prepare you for your next calling.

After all, no one can predict how life will turn out. You can only be certain of the harmony you'll create for yourself and others when your own talents are free to flourish.

Long rows of green seedlings peek out over their tiny pots as hands the color and texture of tree bark tenderly inspect them. The hands belong to a bear of a man clad in rubber boots, dusty work pants, and a blue sweatshirt inscribed "The Herbman."

Leroy Wilton will tell you his mission is simple: to teach others, especially children, how to grow, harvest, and cure with herbs. Aloe and comfrey leaves to heal cuts. Lemon balm to repel mosquitoes. Feverfew for headaches. And the fragrance from a chocolate-scented geranium to ease a young boy's nightmares.

Leroy's fascination with herbs took root while he was working in a steel mill and worrying about inhaling toxins. When a coworker told him that certain natural vitamins help the lungs filter toxins, it opened up a new world to him.

Now he teaches free classes on herbs at the health food store where he tends the Smile-Wilton International Herb Garden, with its more than 275 varieties of herbs from all over the world. In his more modest garden at home, he invites the neighborhood children over to learn firsthand what folk wisdom has known all along— herbs have natural curative powers that are there for the asking, free of charge.

Sometimes when the kids come over, I'll point to "The Herbman" on my shirt and the beeper I wear and ask,

"What does this mean to you?" Usually, they say, "Drug dealer." That's when I say, "I'm here to change that!"

All this started when I used to go out at night after getting off work at the steel mill. I didn't know why, but I was driven to collect old planting pots and trays. I'd think to myself, "What in the world am I going to do with all these things?" But I kept at it anyway.

I knew nothing about herbs at the time. I just started with a small garden with some plants and vegetables. But then when I found out that most of our medicines and vitamins come from plants, I began to learn as much as I could about the human body and how natural plants can do more healing than chemicals and pills.

Without knowing where his drive was coming from, or where it would lead him, Leroy held fast to the belief that he was on the right path. Every day he spent in his makeshift greenhouse, mixing soil or repotting young plants, brought him closer to an inner peace he had never known before and to the unfolding revelation that this was a gift he could share with the world. He says those early days also brought him closer to God.

I started thinking a lot about God and creation. God placed a little bit of cure in every plant on earth, spreading the healing knowledge among all the nations so that everyone would have some. As world neighbors, we would then help one another by sharing the healing powers of our plants.

God could have created a plant that would cure all the diseases in the world, but I guess instead of being grateful we would be trying to sell that plant for thousands of dollars!

This makes sense to me, that this is God's plan and I'm tending one of God's gardens. And the good Lord makes sure that to reach each plant, you have to get down on your knees!

So many of our older people who used herbs as medicines and balms have died, and their knowledge along with them. Someone has to keep that wisdom alive, before it's gone forever. I want my grandchildren to know how to grow and use herbs, so when I leave this life they'll have something to rely on.

While Leroy's calling didn't gel until after retirement, his fascination with nature's growing cycles was something he "knew" early on, as was his strong work ethic.

Growing up, I was always outdoors. I loved the woods—camping and hiking and watching things grow— and there was nothing better than going to my grandmother's house with its fig trees, grapevines, and chickens.

My whole family liked to work as much as we liked to

go camping! Mom cooked at the officers' mess on a military base, and Dad had a bike shop and a confectionery store. When I was only nine, I went out in the neighborhood to shine shoes. In high school I worked part-time—first in a barbershop, then at a dry cleaner's.

I didn't have too many friends in high school—I was the fat boy who stayed by himself. Still, the other kids liked me because they thought I was intelligent. I really was just an average student, but they assumed I was smart because I was quiet.

In most ways, Leroy's childhood was typical—a loving family, a solid education, and plans for the future. But in high school he found out firsthand what it meant to give up a cherished dream simply because of the color of his skin.

As a teenager I wanted to become an FBI agent more than anything. But I was afraid to try because when I was growing up, being black meant that I was limited in what I could dream about. Instead of feeling angry and disappointed, I did what I thought would be the next best thing: I went into the service as soon as I turned eighteen.

I chose the marines because I thought being a marine would be the most challenging thing I could do. There were only two other blacks in my unit. The drill instructors weren't supposed to show prejudice, but they did. Before long, the other two left, and that meant it was just me and seventy-six white guys.

My drill instructor couldn't figure out why this city boy didn't carry a switchblade or get into fights. Even some of my military buddies couldn't figure me out, said I was strange. They expected a certain kind of behavior from me because I was black.

The marines gave me the pay but not the rank—blacks couldn't outrank the white soldiers. It took me thirteen months to get the rank of PFC when it should have taken only six, and then two more years to make corporal.

I didn't like it, but I never let it get to me or give up and become sloppy and disrespectful. When something negative came up, I just went on to something else more positive.

Despite the career limitations forced upon him because of the color of his skin, Leroy blossomed at work, no matter what the job was.

It seemed like whenever I went out for a job, I got it within a couple of weeks. Maybe it was growing up watching my folks work different jobs and teaching the whole family the value of hard work.

When I left the service, I worked at a penitentiary for three years. The pen was segregated, with the white inmates on the upper tier, where they could look out, and the black prisoners on the lower tier, where there were no windows. When the whites were at a table, no blacks could sit there.

After the pen, I went to work in the steel industry and stayed there for the next twenty-six years. Unfortunately, prejudice followed me into the steel mill too. I worked next to a guy eight hours every day for a year, and he never said a word to me. I spent five years sweeping the floor and moving boxes before I got a more permanent job.

Then an opening came up for a ladle man—a very important and dangerous job in a steel mill. If the ladle man can't pour steel into the mold the right way, then nobody gets paid. I applied for the slot and for the next twelve years had to fill in as a temporary ladle man before I got the permanent position. But I didn't lose hope or get down about it. I just kept at it, doing the best job possible.

Then in the 1970s, the federal government made it mandatory that companies place more black supervisors in managerial positions. I was working a Class 5 job and this new managerial position was paying Class 21. So I said, "Sure, why not?"

But the steel mill only saw me as a token. Management just didn't get it, that this energetic young black man would be good for the company. So you know what I did? I made sure I was the best token manager they ever had!

My coworkers sometimes called me counterfeit because I wasn't what they thought I should be—hollering, screaming, and cursing just like them. But I wasn't like that. I just went about my business. I took pride in my work, whatever it was, and knew things would get better, no matter how long it took. And eventually those men at the steel mill who wouldn't speak to me, over time I turned them around.

And while money was important to put food on the table for my family, it was never the main motivation in my work. It was the challenge to do something better, to be the best at what I did. I was the best ladle man in the shop and the best manager.

While a career in the steel mill was a far cry from Leroy's initial dream of joining the FBI, his love of nature never left him. Over the years, he began gardening in his spare time and rediscovered the joy he had felt as a young boy in the woods watching things grow.

After work I puttered around in my makeshift greenhouse and garden at home. I used to scrounge up anything I could find to bring it back to my greenhouse—old plastics, windows, flowerpots, and trays—all kinds of treasures.

Then I'd go over to the local Kmart, fish out the thrown-away plants from the Dumpster, and treat them with manure and organic mixes so they'd come back beautiful. I started experimenting with growing techniques. I used classical music and lights at night with my plants. Did you know you can hear corn growing at night? It crackles!

Before long the house was full of plants. My wife, Ida, suggested that we set up a plant stand and sell some of them. One day a fellow walked up to the stand, and we ended up talking about religion. While we talked, no one drove by, no horns honked; it was quiet. He offered to come back in a week to talk to me again. I went inside and told Ida, "I don't know what it is, hon, but I feel different."

Everybody already assumed I was religious—I was ethical and tried to live right, but I couldn't say I really knew God. But that day I must have been looking for something more in my life. I felt comfortable with this man and somehow knew that the time had come to learn about God. So he started coming over to the house to teach me, and I became more and more hungry to learn.

I was baptized at a church where I was the only black member. I was saved in a white church!

One of my favorite church activities was what I call the Safeway Food Ministry. I drove my van to the local Safeway stores to pick up their extra food, then deliver it to different places like senior citizen centers and nursing homes. Sometimes I'd be riding on Jesus gas. I'd say, "Oh, Lord, I'm on empty, but please just get me to the next stop." And I always made it.

Leroy might not have known it at the time, but his gift of making the best of every situation and his willingness to walk through the doors that opened to him—even the ones he thought he didn't want—brought him closer to his calling.

My lifelong curiosity about growing things kept pushing me—God was the driving force behind that. No matter how hard work was or what kind of mood I was in, once I came out to my greenhouse and started working with the plants, I'd be fine again.

That's when I knew that herb gardening was my calling. And you know what? Whatever I needed, I was provided.

People have told me that I could make more money if I grew flowers or expanded my business, but I know now that my purpose is to teach others about herbs, not make money from them.

Because it's what I'm supposed to be doing, I feel like nothing can stop me. Even on a day when I have to do something boring, like repot all my stock plants, I stay focused and don't drift off, no matter how tired I get. And I feel at peace. Besides, God lets me know when it's time to rest—my legs will act up or I'll start wobbling around my greenhouse!

This is what God has taught me through my herbs: You have to constantly give to others to make more room inside. One day at the shop where I sell my herbs, a young girl was walking around in the garden studying the plants. So I said hello and we started talking. She asked me to tell her about the aloe plant. I explained it was good for acne and showed her how to use it. Then I gave it to her, but made her promise to share it with her brother. She couldn't believe it. "For me?" she asked. "Free?" Well, her parents couldn't believe it either, that I would just give this plant to their daughter! But I know she'll never forget the day she first learned about the aloe and what it's used for. She'll be able to pass that information on to others. See how it works?

4

Find Your Home

I personally couldn't survive wondering if I should have done it. I would much rather do it and fail. And there's a lot of potential to fail. But then again, it might turn out to be something I'd enjoy. I'm lucky in this case.

MARY DISANZA

45, Dive Store Manager

Conventional wisdom would tell us that no matter where we go, we can never truly leave ourselves behind. We take the same baggage of problems, the same bad habits and attitudes, the same perspectives that made us who we were at our former address. Therefore, the reasoning goes, there's no point in moving. Just stay home and stick it out.

Not true. Many calling-seekers must find the right environment that will allow them to fully express themselves.

Perhaps it's the climate. Perhaps it's a community of kindred spirits. The city. The country. The mountains. The water.

Home is where you can be yourself. And you must be yourself to fully achieve your potential and express your gifts.

Look at the map of the Western Hemisphere and find Venezuela. Trace your finger along the coastline and up into the Caribbean Sea. A little to the right of Maracaibo you'll see a pinprick. This is the island of Bonaire, a land of flamingos, salt flats, iguanas, parrots, and natural preserves, both above the water and below it. This is the home of Mary DiSanza, a Colorado native who came for a vacation, stayed, and blossomed.

You can find Mary at the Sunset Beach Hotel dive shop. On the surface hers is a world of sounds: the squawking of the two parrots in the cage next to the sliding glass door of the store; the squawking of the T-shirted tourists trying to get the parrots to talk back; Dutch, English, Spanish, and the island language, Papiamento; the clink of hundreds of scuba tanks as they rattle against each other like milk bottles; and the quiet hum of diesel engines as they carry divers to some of the world's best dive locations.

Mary is equally at home below the water, where with one splashy giant stride she enters a world in which the muffled chips and clicks of life on the coral reef replace the clattery noises from above. Velvety blue tangs, rainbow-colored parrot fish snoozing in the protective shelter of their own mucus bubble, feisty angelfish, and curious barracuda, sleek as jets, might notice as she glides by. But they quickly return to their own business, or perhaps follow her for a while, nipping at her fin tips.

As a dive shop manager, her job is to make tourists happy. Her calling is to make them happy on Bonaire. Because Bonaire is where she herself can be truly happy.

It means a lot to have someone come in specifically to say, "Hey, we had a great time. You guys have the best job in the world." That's great to me because vacations should be fantasies for people. They shouldn't see how hard you've worked. They shouldn't see the behind-the-scenes things. They shouldn't see us hauling two hundred scuba tanks. They shouldn't see us crawling around the bilge repairing a boat. They shouldn't see the time we were out here at three in the morning getting the boats out of the water because a ferocious storm was developing.

If they leave here thinking we have a great life down here and that everything is just perfect, well, then, maybe they've relaxed. You can't ask for more than that.

We're probably luckier than most people. When folks are on holiday, they're already pretty good-natured.

They're ready to have a good time—they paid good money for it.

When people come into my shop grouchy, I'll do everything short of standing on my head to get them to crack a grin. Sometimes I can't, but usually you can gently poke people out of a bad mood.

Mary's journey to Bonaire started in Colorado, where she grew up horseback riding and shooting trap. The oldest of three children, she was raised with a sense of unlimited possibilities and a unisex work ethic—two qualities that quickly made her an outsider in her own neighborhood. She would never again experience the same culture shock that she faced when she first tried out her parents' teachings on her immediate world.

Our parents were always there when we needed them, but they realized early on that they wouldn't always be there for us. So they decided they had better raise some freethinkers. Looking back, I realize that we all had a lot more freedom than a lot of the other kids. If we ever had a problem or a situation that confused us, we only had to ask our parents for help. But they did steer us toward trying to solve our own problems first.

We had no women's work or men's work. Both our parents worked outside the home, and they both did work in the house. I used to tease my father that he created a monster because I didn't know what "women's work" was. My parents told me I could do anything I wanted, as long as I had the strength and the mentality for it.

It came as a culture shock that there were people out there who segregated jobs. I remember thinking how hard it was to fit into the rest of the world, because my friends didn't feel the same way about work that I did. To me it was always the best person who should do the job. If you're good at what you do, then go do it.

If you're great at brain surgery, but you can't add 2 and 4, then you should be in the operating room. But you shouldn't be balancing your family's finances.

The same goes for fun. I did lots of non-girl sports, but in retrospect I now see that I didn't know it at the time. The children used to bird-dog for my father, but I never took any pleasure in killing anything. I enjoyed shooting trap and skeet. That's a lot of fun, and if I missed, I didn't have to wring something's neck because it wasn't dead.

About the same time I used to come home from school and watch *Sea Hunt*. Good old Mike Nelson did everything wrong. He used to take people back into the water to decompress them. He'd put his mask on top of his head, which is an instant sign of distress. But it was so much fun to watch that I decided then that someday I wanted to learn to dive. And that was in the days of black-and-white television! You couldn't even see the colors that are underwater.

For a while I thought it would be fun to be a marine biologist, until I found out that a lot of marine biologists ended up as cooks on sailboats. There aren't a tremendous number of jobs for marine biologists. But I still regret not getting the education. I would have learned a lot more.

Mary's first taste of real adventure came when she boarded a plane to Germany to marry her high school sweetheart, who was stationed there with the army. She was only eighteen. Her new husband would show a distaste for flying and travel. She, on the other hand, discovered wells of resourcefulness and an eagerness to meet new people at every turn.

My mother was in tears and figured I was going off the end of the earth. Dad was really cool about it, saying, "You're going to do what you want anyway. It will sort itself out." He would say something like that again twenty years later.

Since my husband worked during the day, I was all by myself most of the time. But it was fine and I was never homesick. It was an adventure. I'd go out every single day and try to learn to do the shopping the way the German ladies do it. I went on walking tours of the little village I lived in. One day my husband came home with an international driver's license for me. My first day out in our little Volkswagen I had an accident. Of all the cars I had to hit, it had to be a Mercedes.

I'm nosy. The more you can learn about a place, the more fun it is. I've traveled with some groups, but I value the times I've traveled by myself more. You learn so much more that way. When you have a little core group, you're tempted to cling to it. Consequently it's possible to go to several islands or countries and know nothing about them by the time you get home.

I found I would make more friends and know more about where I went when I traveled alone. Eventually you would have to talk to a stranger, and sometimes you would hit it off and make new friends.

Upon their return, the marriage began a long, slow decline. And Mary discovered her ongoing need to travel, to learn, and to expose herself to new experiences. The more she explored the world, the more she realized that home was where she wasn't at home anymore.

I changed jobs every two years. Once there's no more to learn, the job stops being fun. It seems in some areas of corporate life, people jealously guard what they do. Maybe they're afraid that once you learn everything you'll take their job. But I found over and over again that I could learn only so much at each job. When I couldn't learn any more and no one was willing to share any more knowledge, that's usually the point when I left for something else.

I did everything from statistical typing to banking. It was when I worked for a maxilla-oral facial surgeon that I started talking with a friend there about *Sea Hunt*. I think I must have had a book with me about whales and dolphins. Turns out she'd always wanted to learn how to dive, too, so we agreed to learn together.

It was terrible. There we were in a cold swimming pool in the middle of winter in Denver. The instructor was awful, and I never knew what he wanted from us. I decided that diving had to be a lot better than this, and if I could get out of the swimming pool and into an ocean somewhere I'd be fine.

The magic part came when I did my open-water certification dive in the British Virgin Islands. Once we were underwater I was amazed at how pretty it all was. It was so lush, so gorgeous. My instructor had to shake me to get me to pay attention to her and demonstrate my skills.

I hated to leave. I really enjoy the islands. And I love warm weather. I love the palm trees and the ocean. The more I traveled to the Caribbean, the harder and harder it was to go back. It would take longer and longer to get back into the mode of getting into my car and driving to work.

It would also take Mary longer and longer to return to her marriage. And eventually they agreed to end the marriage and remain friends. As one relationship ended, another began to bloom.

I was wishing more and more that I lived on an island and didn't have to come back home. And I'm sure he got used to me being gone. He's such a good man, and he did his very best to take care of me. But we just grew apart as we grew up.

After I left my husband, I met Walter through diving. We hit it off and started talking about how we went to the Caribbean so much that we might as well live there. That was my bright idea, and I've been blamed for it ever since.

Walter mentioned Bonaire as a possibility. I had never been here, but he had. And he knew it was safe and the people were very friendly. Best of all, the reefs had been protected since 1976. It was all marine park and in pretty good shape.

So we came down on holiday and brought a stack of résumés. There were five hotels on the island at the time that ran dive shops. But they weren't looking for anyone. A big drawback for us was our lack of languages. They really do prefer people who can speak at least two or three languages. But we passed around our résumés all over the island anyway.

One day we happened to run into Anton, who owns the

dive shop at the hotel right where we were staying. We had been looking all around, not knowing that right in front of our nose the shop needed a couple who could manage it.

Couples, by the way, do much better on islands. There aren't a lot of people in the social pool. We finally got a movie theater, but otherwise there's not much else here. So employers like couples because they have each other. They'll last longer than most people. It's also cheaper for a couple to live down here with two salaries to depend on.

Single women do better also. They're usually used to taking care of themselves. The worst off are the single guys. They typically can't cook or take care of themselves domestically. They usually last the shortest amount of time, unless they end up with a wife or girlfriend—in which case they end up in the couple mode and do really well.

So we agreed to work with Anton and went back home to put things in storage and wrap up our lives there. Once again, my dad said that things would work themselves out.

I know it sounded like I was planning to run off and join the circus. It doesn't sound like the brightest idea in the world, and I'm sure that to a lot of people it sounds like career suicide. I personally couldn't survive wondering if I should have done it. I would much rather do it and fail.

And there's a lot of potential to fail. But then again, it might turn out to be something I'd enjoy. I'm lucky in this case.

I'm asked all the time if I had second thoughts about the life I was leaving behind. But people who really do something like this usually don't think that way. If you think, "Oh, my God, I'm leaving my house, I'm leaving my cars, my life," you won't be going anyway.

But for me the right cars and the right clothes had gotten old. I found that in my old life a lot of self-worth was based on what you materially possessed. But I was never really that way. A big storm can come through and take everything you own. But it wouldn't make you any less of a person.

So you do what you must do to make it happen. And then you go.

You do it up front, and you do it open. You tell your friends, "I have to try it." You have to give it 110 percent. You better try, and you better give it everything you've got.

You're probably better off even if you do it and you fall flat on your face. Okay. That doesn't mean you're stupid or wrong. It just means that wasn't the lifestyle for you. But at least you tried.

Life on Bonaire carries with it a whole new set of challenges. And Mary entered this new life knowing that it wasn't going to be an end-

less summer vacation. Things don't happen as rapidly as they do in the United States. Vital paperwork may take more time going through the bureaucracies. Houses take longer to be built. The precious water hookup may or may not happen by the time you're ready to move in. The supermarket shelves are stocked with whatever happens to have arrived in the port that week. Bonaire depends on the containers that arrive via ships steaming in and out of its little harbor. Those containers carry Mary's new oak kitchen cabinets from Washington State, or hundreds of boxes of Wheaties for the supermarket. Whatever it is, if it doesn't come out of a container, it probably comes out of a friend's suitcase. Or you don't get it. Bonaire depends on its links to the outside world that much.

And the residents of Bonaire depend on each other just as heavily. On such a small island everyone knows who to turn to for expert help. Mary knows the optometrist who can advise you on the wisdom of diving with a detached retina. She knows who to turn to for help with the boat electronics. And she knows the lady who specializes in rehabilitating the wild flamingos that get injured during their daily commute from Venezuela to Bonaire. And every once in a while a diver will come through who knows about caring for the two parrots that keep watch by the dive shop's rinse tank. And she knows the dive shop managers up and down the island. Even though they're competitors, they are also partners in a way that no mainland chamber of commerce could imagine.

There are a lot of nice people who will help. We're all

different but we all work together. Make no mistake, we're all in business. And we're not going to be really really close friends, because business comes first. But we also work as a team because it's for the betterment of Bonaire.

If our compressor breaks, I guarantee you we can count on the other shops. And vice versa. If one of the other shops' compressor breaks, we'll fill those tanks and we won't charge them. Those tanks will go out on their boats, and their divers will dive, have a great time, and never know the difference.

It's better to help your competitor send those people home with good memories. That way the whole island will have a good reputation.

All the dive shop managers get together once a month to talk over concerns and ways we can help each other and the island in general. All the dive shops have worked in the Bonaire Marine Park to teach the local children how to snorkel and take care of the beauty that they have. We draw our living from the island; it's only right that we should give something back.

This is great for me because I've been wishing there was something I could do. The people our age grew up on Bonaire not knowing how to swim because their parents wouldn't let them near the water. But they don't want their own children to grow up that way. I think this would be a great thing to do for the island. And I would like to take it further by showing the children the different things they can see underwater and explain fish behavior. But my Papiamentu needs to be better if I want to be able to talk with the littlest kids.

Diving is still so special to me that I want to share the underwater world as much as I can. Even though I run the shop and don't dive with the guests so much anymore, I'll still grab a tank and just go cruising for relaxation. It's so peaceful and tranquil for me. When I come up is a great time to ask me for money.

When I have a terrible day, I can go diving, and all those things that I thought were so terrible take a backseat. When I get out of the water, things just don't seem as bad as they were.

Just as Mary's parents taught her to decide for herself what kind of life she wanted to make, Mary eventually introduced to them the life she did make far away from Colorado. After ushering hundreds of divers through the waters surrounding Bonaire, she was able to share with her mother and father the world she loves beneath the water's surface.

The year before my father died, Mom and Dad came down to visit me. Mom is so sweet but hates the heat. And she's not a good swimmer, so she was uncomfortable in the water. So I was really touched when she gamely stood in the water right off the beach, with her mask on, peering directly down at the fish.

But Dad. He had a ball. He was out there for two hours, snorkeling all around the dock and watching all the fish. Every once in a while you could hear him coughing and sputtering and laughing. He'd get so absorbed watching the fish that he'd forget you can't breathe under water.

When he came out, he was so happy. He kept saying, "Thank you, thank you for giving me that. I never dreamed it was possible."

I still miss him a lot.

5

Follow Your Interests

All of my interests seemed to take me in different, random directions. I felt like I was walking a drunkard's walk, but it was really a straight line.

BARRY ARMOUR

49, Head of Technical Directors, Industrial Light & Magic

Think back to when you were a child. What interests did you have? What activities kept you happily occupied for hours, oblivious to the outside world?

Many of us are first introduced to lifelong passions when we're young, perhaps in the form of a hobby that transcends childlike curiosity. And when we become adults, some of us continue to pursue those cherished activities, turning them into our life's work.

But many of us regard our interests as only a sideline, a distraction from the demands of what we think is our more serious work. In this society, an outside pursuit doesn't have the same value as a job title, salary, or professional status.

And yet your interests are a direct reflection of who you are and what you love to do best. Follow them. They'll lead you directly to your calling.

Located in a nondescript industrial park in northern California, George Lucas's Industrial Light & Magic is where many of the special effects you see in films are created on computers and soundstages. The back lot is reserved for more explosive outdoor stuff, like the crash landing of the starship Enterprise *in the movie* Generations. *Other tenants in the park don't seem to mind the occasional fireworks coming from their neighbor.*

While there's nothing elaborate about the entrance and reception area, human traffic does pass by two very familiar screen characters—Darth Vader and R2D2, life-size props from the Star Wars *film trilogy. Walking through Industrial Light & Magic is like winding through a rabbit's warren—a maze of cubbyhole offices adorned with movie posters, movie memorabilia, and little toys perched on desks and computer equipment. The air is filled with a kind of youthful creativity.*

One of the people in charge of this creativity is Barry Armour. He may be forty-nine, but he'll tell you that working for George Lucas is like being a kid again. Barry and his staff add all the gee-whiz special effects to a story that make it burst with heart-thumping life on the big screen. Casper. Dragonheart. *The much-anticipated newest installment of* Star Wars.

Fun? You bet. But the work is also demanding and oftentimes grueling. It's not unusual for Barry's team to put in long hours during a project, but he says that's just part of the painstaking art of making movie magic. As long as it looks perfect on the screen, no one needs to know how much effort went into the process.

I look back at how I got to where I am now and can't help but think of a mathematical expression I learned in school—the drunkard's walk. It's a randomized movement in a certain direction where it doesn't appear that you're going from point A to point B.

That's been my life. All of my interests seemed to take me in different, random directions. I felt like I was walking a drunkard's walk, but it was really a straight line.

I remember seeing *Star Wars* when it first came out in the late seventies and thinking, "It would be neat to work for George Lucas, but I'm just a regular guy. I run a computer graphics business and don't know anything about special effects in the movies."

Today I've just come from a meeting at ILM where I've

seen the storyboards for the next *Star Wars* series, and they're unbelievable! The movie will be unlike anything we've seen before!

Barry's childlike fascination is a trait he remembers having early on in life, a trait he explored freely through a number of interests.

When I was a young boy I was fascinated by rocket propulsion and wanted to be a nuclear physicist. In high school I became really interested in chemistry, thanks to a great chemistry teacher.

Parallel to this was my deep and abiding interest in photography. When I was eleven, business friends of my parents gave me their outdated photography equipment. That started my experimentation, playing around with developing my own pictures and rotting out our aluminum ice-cube trays in the process! By high school I was making money taking sports pictures.

I also grew up listening to my father play jazz piano and learned to play myself. I had a passion for reading science fiction—again, the influence of my father, who read the greats like Heinlein, Norton, and E. E. Smith.

In college, Barry chose biochemistry as his major, but noticed something odd his junior year. He looked around physical chemistry class and didn't know anyone. But in the philosophy class he was taking, he knew everyone. It wasn't that chemistry wasn't interesting, it was just that he enjoyed his nondegree courses more.

I looked at my fellow students in chemistry and asked myself, "Do I really want to spend all of my time with these people?" My answer was that I'd rather be a photographer, so I switched from a bachelor of science to a bachelor of arts.

My senior year was a lot of fun—I studied classical guitar and built a darkroom in a friend's basement.

I also was a rock 'n' roll musician; I played in a group with my friends. My parents told me they were hoping I would be more serious instead of living the life of a scruffy hippie. But, hey, I could still string two sentences together! In fact, I learned a lot about electronics, from playing rock 'n' roll to building my own fuzz tones (sound modifiers) to working with the sound equipment, which was always breaking down.

You see, my interests really drove me. If something felt right and I thought I could do it, then nothing could stop me from trying. And failure didn't bother me as long as I was learning.

While taking a night course in photography, Barry accepted a job as an assistant photographer with the instructor's studio. A while later he was laid off when the photo department closed because the studio wasn't doing well.

The studio was trying to drum up business in what we used to call multimedia. My former boss there called me and asked if I wanted to join another company and learn multimedia. (Until computer video displays came on the scene, businesses relied on slide shows for their presentations.) I became pretty adept at editing visuals and producing sound tracks.

The skills I developed at the studio helped me land a job as an audiovisual producer for Bell of Pennsylvania in one of the Executive Communication Centers. I had a certain amount of creative control at the center and was part of an enthusiastic group. Our motto was "Whatever it takes."

But we were spending a lot of money on graphics and montages, and I suggested we buy an optical camera so that we could do the work in-house and save money. This was in the late seventies, and no one was doing anything really innovative with motion graphics; it was still mostly static-looking graphics slides. I remember going to a presentation where someone did a kind of rip-off *Star Wars* special effect, and I thought, "Now, that's neat!" I wanted to be able to do those special effects.

I began programming shows on the side and, over time, built up a demand for my motion graphics work. No one else was doing it, so I sank my money into a huge motion graphics camera and went into business for myself. Then the medium exploded!

I loved running my own graphics business. It did so well

that my former boss became one of my biggest clients. The only part of the business I hated was the administrative stuff.

In 1991 the recession hit. As businesses reined in what they could spend on multimedia projects, Barry began to lose clients. Worse yet, he had to lay off employees. That part of the job was so painful that sometimes he kept people on for months after he should have let them go.

For the next few years he worked at a negative salary, picking up freelance assignments wherever he could. For the most part, he and his wife, Margaret, lived on her salary.

Then an anonymous guardian angel paved the way for Barry's new life, although, to this day, he's still not sure who it was.

I was miserable. For three straight years my business lost money. One of the employees I had to lay off kept in touch with me after he went to work for a modeling-animation software firm called Alias. When the company had an opening in Los Angeles, I applied for it, but nothing came of it.

I think it was the L.A. office of Alias that sent my résumé on to George Lucas, who was looking for a modeler at the time. The day before Thanksgiving I got a call from ILM about my résumé, but I didn't hear anything after our initial talk and thought, Oh, well, that's the way it goes. In mid-January ILM called again. This time the company was looking for technical directors. After a few phone interviews, ILM wanted to fly me out to California for a visit.

Suddenly it was scary, because Margaret and I liked Philadelphia and had a close circle of friends and business contacts there. I asked the folks at ILM to fly both my wife and me out, and they said fine. I wanted her to go because if I was offered a job, then we could make the decision together.

The visit showed me that ILM was the embodiment of everything I was looking for! George Lucas had built a company that nurtured creative energy. People were coming to ILM from all over the world—sometimes at a salary reduction—just to learn from the best minds in digital graphics and special effects.

Barry and Margaret did some soul-searching and came to the same conclusion: an opportunity like this might not come around again. They decided to take the plunge and move lock, stock, and barrel to the West Coast. Margaret stayed back in Philadelphia for the next six months to sell their house and tie up loose ends where she worked. Barry rented a small apartment down the hill from Lucas's 4,700-acre Skywalker Ranch—another creativity-enhancing work environment with its offices and studios tucked in among rolling hills, vineyards, and winding trails.

At first I was hired as a technical director, partly because the company was worried that I didn't have enough experience in managing people. In other words, I hadn't shown my chops. But there was room for advancement, and since most of ILM's new employees were in their twenties and thirties, I had the advantage of having more seasoned business experience as well as technological knowledge.

I was disappointed that I wouldn't be making the salary I did during the good years of running my own business, but I had also just been through three bad years!

Barry's diverse interests in science, science fiction, photography, and computer graphics magically came together under one roof. It was his willingness to follow those interests—throughout his life— that finally brought him clear across the country in pursuit of his destiny.

I've had a lot to learn over the last few years—the film industry has its own technological quirks—but many of the techniques are the same as what I used back east. Besides, it's interesting keeping up with the technological changes. For example, just a few years ago everyone used the optical printer for special effects. Then digital came along. Lucas shut down ILM's entire optical department and offered the employees there the opportunity to be retrained in the new digital technology.

I think about those pioneers in movie technology who created the special effects in the original *Star Wars*, and now that technology is obsolete. They developed what was state-of-the-art for that era in motion pictures and then created their own unemployment when the technology changed. Meanwhile I was still in Philadelphia running my computer graphics business, but making a point of staying one step ahead of the technology.

The digital special effects you see today—Lucas is responsible for most of the key innovations. Essentially ILM seeded the special effects industry. In fact, former ILM employees have gone on to start their own digital effects companies.

Barry has taken on more of a people-management role at ILM, with the understanding that he will keep a hand in production. He often acts as a mentor to the younger employees as they learn how to translate imaginative creations into real screen images.

We're not the storytellers, but the special effects are very much a part of the storytelling process. ILM wants individuals who are willing to learn the proprietary software and fit into the culture here. That's why I'm more interested in hiring for temperament than for skills.

For me, the most exciting aspect is working with the people I see in movie credits, the very best in the business. I can't say how long I'll be at ILM, but I know I'm having too much fun to see myself retiring!

Someday I would like to do some visual effects supervision. But, you know, as long as I can do what I enjoy doing, then I can be happy anywhere.

Part Two

BUILD YOUR CALLING

Everyone starts from scratch. Even the geniuses.
Remember, even Mozart had teachers.
Patiently construct your calling with the finest
materials: a bright, open, and creative mind; kind and
generous teachers; loving and supportive friends and
family; and the time you need to get it right.
And aim for the best you can imagine. Time and
persistence will make your dreams come true. So be
sure to make them high-quality dreams.

6

Commit Yourself to a Lifetime of Learning

If I can only see something from one point of view,
I automatically think I'm missing something.

SAM HOERTER

41, Airport Director

Because your calling is never intended to be a final destination, it can be better described as your path toward fulfilling your potential and making the world a better place.

For this you need help; you must be willing to ask the giants if you can stand on their shoulders. To ask questions, to learn, and to change your mind as you go along. For many people, like Sam Hoerter, the first step on his calling path was the question "What are you doing?" Followed by his next step, the question "Why are you doing that?" Followed by the next step, the question "What are you going to do next?"

Don't be afraid to ask questions. And be willing to patiently teach in return. Those are your steps toward your future.

When you think about careers in aviation, the obvious jobs immediately come to mind: pilot, flight attendant, baggage handler. But flights begin and end at airports, and airports are like big cities. They have their own stores and restaurants and their own real estate. They often have their own police and fire departments; they have their own roads and sidewalks and parking. And they have their own laws. Every day hundreds of thousands of people depend on at least two airports to run smoothly for them—the one they left and the one they're going to.

So, airports, like cities, need their own manager, the individual who understands every detail of the way an airport is run and is able to make literally life-and-death decisions on the spot. Airport directors must be politically talented to work effectively with local and federal politicians. They must be entrepreneurs in order to raise millions of dollars every year to keep their facilities safe and efficient.

They must be flexible and philosophical, because a lot happens at airports every day, and not all of it goes according to plan.

Like most airport directors, Sam Hoerter entered the profession because he was attracted to the planes. But he stays in the profession because he cares about the people. The director of a medium-sized southern airport, he started his career on a fluke and then discovered that this was a job where the old-timers would answer a young college kid's questions. And then answer some more.

And so he stayed, becoming at twenty-eight one of the youngest airport directors in U.S. history, which many who know his warmth, genuine nature, and passion for learning would agree was his destiny. And there are others who know his tendency to use colorful words to describe the bureaucratic and political nonsense he must deal with. Those are the people who might call his career a miracle.

But at first it wasn't destiny or a miracle. He just wanted a job to help pay his way through college.

I grew up as an air force brat and spent a lot of time around airplanes. I liked them, but I never thought I'd work around them. I didn't know what I was going to be when I grew up; I was having too much fun being a kid to worry about what kind of job I was going to have.

But because I moved around a lot, I grew to be very comfortable with change—a lot more so than the average person, I guess. That's become an advantage in the kind of work I do today because I'm able to walk into unfamiliar situations and not be uncomfortable with that.

But by the time I was in college, I was failing out of engineering. And one Monday morning I decided to change my curriculum. So I simply went through the college catalog looking for majors that didn't require calculus, physics, or chemistry. I was still in the A's when I hit aviation management. On Tuesday I walked into the co-op office and said, "I need a job. I'm an aviation management student as of yesterday."

They had two interviews scheduled for that week. One was with an airport; the other was with a start-up cargo company that was flying cargo around in small jets. I decided that was too radical an idea for me and that that company wouldn't last long. So I passed up an interview with Federal Express and took the airport job.

Tells you what a visionary I am.

By taking an administrative assistant job at the Birmingham, Alabama, airport, Sam suddenly found himself the youngest of a group of people in which the second-youngest was fifty-nine years old.

One of the advantages of being a kid was that they all took me in as their pet. Being naturally curious, I bothered everybody. I'd ask everyone, "What are you doing? Why are you doing that?" And they enjoyed showing me.

My work schedule wasn't rigid and I could get my responsibilities done in thirty minutes. Then I'd hop on the truck with the maintenance crew and say, "How do you patch a concrete hole? Show me. Why did you do it that way?" At some point I'm sure I must have infuriated some people, and they'd toss me out, saying, "Leave me alone." But I don't remember who those people were. Most of them were very happy to take me along and show me what they did.

The maintenance superintendent, a fellow named Al Schmidt, never got disgusted with me. I think he actually got a kick out of me; he couldn't believe that a boy from college could be so stupid. He was a lot of fun and would not only answer all my questions, but he'd go the next logical step.

I had a lot of kindness around me. The people I worked with were some of the most honest and decent and regular kinds of guys that you'd ever want to meet. Of course, eventually I learned that the whole world is not like that. But that first crew I was thrown in with were just decent human beings.

I just assumed all airports were like that. Full of people who want to answer a kid's questions.

And, of course, there were the planes. I really enjoy them, how they move and how they work. Just getting the food on an airplane sounds boring, but to watch how they do it, how their work needs to be choreographed, is really interesting. When you get underneath the belly of a plane and watch everyone moving around, it's astonishing.

So eventually Sam stopped watching the technology and began watching the people. And his professional life began there.

I became more interested in the people, how the relationships are balanced so that all of them get their work done in the time and the space they need and with the battle between chaos and order that exists everywhere.

Every time a plane crashes, people say, "How could this happen?" And all I can say is "Why doesn't this happen every moment?" It's amazing to me how humans overcome our natural weaknesses. When you think how easy it is to miscommunicate, how easy it is to misplace something. And no human being goes to work and performs 100 percent perfectly every day.

When a person comes in to work after having had a fight with his wife that morning and is feeling poorly, how does he overcome all that to move a plane 500 miles an hour to within a half inch of where it's supposed to stop? That happens a gazillion times every day.

And you can't order everything. If you get too anal and try to write the procedure for everything, it stops. It just doesn't work. And so there has to be this blend of "Here's what you do, here's kind of how you do it, and your creativity has to come into play as you do what you're supposed to do. And yet your own way can't be too far out of bounds. And we're counting on you to concentrate while you're doing it."

I'm taking things less and less for granted every year.

After graduation, Sam was hired at the same airport as operations manager, replacing a World War I veteran who finally retired. After five years he became the director of a small airport in Gulfport, Mississippi, at twenty-eight years old. His own youth didn't intimidate him. He just asked for help. All the time. And, he reasoned, if he failed totally he was still young enough to start a new career.

I've never been one to worry about screwing up. We all screw up. If you don't screw up, you're not working. In a way, I was all alone, but again I was also surrounded by good people.

If you have people around you who just want to cut your throat, you're not going to get anywhere. Fortunately, I worked with people who were comfortable with me, even though they were old enough to be my mother or father. I'd just say up front, "You've got to help me," and damned if they didn't.

I would say, "I've got this great idea!" just like the boss in the Dilbert comic. And they would say, "That's dumb as hell, boy. That's not going to work." And then they'd tell me why, and they were right. And I'd learn something.

One of the advantages of being a kid is that people treated me with the disrespect I deserved. One of the disadvantages of getting older is that people start treating you with respect that you don't deserve.

As you get older and your hair goes away or gets gray, and you wear a starched white shirt, and you throw out some idea and everybody says, "That's a great idea, boss!" and you say to yourself, "Oh, God, what have I done?"

Unfortunately, Sam's strength in accepting criticism was also his weakness in delivering it. But then again, the kindness and patience of an older employee helped Sam see the world through the eyes of others.

Early on, I'd assume other people were the same way I was. When I got to be someone's boss, I'd walk into their office and say, "I need this, this, and this. And you screwed up this, this, and this. Bye." Then I'd come back ten minutes later and see that person sobbing at his desk and wonder why. I just didn't get it.

It took a while for me to realize that not everyone views the world as I do. Some people realize that when they're five or six. It took me a lot longer. But as I've come to realize that, I've discovered that (a) it's a lot of fun, because it's a source of new information for me, and (b) it's the essence of what politics is all about.

I'm not only hearing what the person says but trying to really feel it. Now if I can only see something from one point of view, I automatically think I'm missing something.

Then it came to me one morning. One of the airport staff members, Fred Chapin, made a comment one day that his daughter had just had a birthday and that she was the same age as me. Then he said, "I might have passed you in a hall somewhere when your mother was carrying you out in a blanket."

He was the man who answered my questions. I'd go out and do something wrong, and he'd take me aside and say, "Come here. That's not going to work. You can't treat people like that."

If there had been ill will in his heart, he would have sat back and watched me screw up by doing it my way, and then thought how smart he was and what a schmuck I was.

When I first started coming to this realization, one of the things I would do is come to work in the morning before anyone was there. And I'd use my master key to go into their office and sit at their desk and put myself in their position: "I am old enough to be my boss's father. What do

I feel like sitting in this chair?" Every morning I would put myself in someone else's chair and learn how they might view things differently.

A father himself, Sam is now looking at the world through his son's eyes as well. And part of that process is letting Joseph come to work and sit at his desk and look out his father's big window as the jets land and take off again and again all day long.

We all have a moral obligation to bring up the next generation. Frequently he'd come out here and play on the computer, or we'd hop in a golf cart, crawl in a cockpit, or go get a plane and go flying. He gets this impression that all I do is play all day.

I tell him that mostly what I do is make choices. Everybody else has a job except for me. I'm the one who has to make the choices. We either do it this way or that way. We have a dollar to spend. Do we buy a flak jacket or a telephone? Someone has to make the call.

Another choice for Sam is the choice of what his job means to him.

Early on, my attitude was that people are here to serve the airport, to make this marvelous machine, this invention of humankind, work. Now it's flipped. All of this is a marvelous tool for human development. It makes people feel good to be a part of something that not everyone can be a part of.

Here if you make a mistake you're generally forgiven. If you make two mistakes in a row, that's when bad things happen. Think about a job where you have to score better than 98 percent every day. That's tough.

If we can get people working together, sharing, and being honest with each other, not being ashamed to make a mistake, to laugh at themselves, and to cover for each other, that's a marvelous tool for making people feel good about themselves.

I get to see it all happen, to see it all work out here. People say I have the best view in town with these big windows looking out over the runways. But I hardly look out the window anymore. My view is out the door toward my employees.

7

Take It One Step
at a Time

*It's like there's a golden cloud hanging over
us. What we set out to do, we achieve. It's like the
roadblocks aren't even there anymore.*

KEN AND ELLEN KAYE

50, Owners, Woodwind Sail Charter Operation

Turning your calling into a working reality takes more than
passion. It requires a careful, coolheaded process from start
to finish. And the patience to do whatever must be done,
however long it takes, to reach your goal.

Never lose sight of the fact that you are building your
life's work. Your calling deserves everything you have to
give.

Cutting through the waters of the Chesapeake Bay is the 74-foot schooner Woodwind. *Her sails full, she's running with the wind, and everyone on board—her captain, Ken Kaye, the crew, and forty or so passengers—is sharing that same sense of giddy freedom* Woodwind *always seems to unleash.*

Equal parts skipper, teacher, and entertainer, the wiry Ken Kaye is right at home on deck. One minute he's recruiting volunteers to take a turn at the wheel. The next he's singing sea chanteys—or show tunes—whatever it takes to make every sailing excursion an unforgettable experience for all aboard.

Back in the office, Ellen Kaye captains her own journey through the business waters of Woodwind Sail Charter Operation. A self-proclaimed type A personality, she welcomes the daily challenge of navigating her way through the forms and figures of a thriving sail charter business.

Together this former teaching couple literally built their dream come true, the schooner Woodwind. *Using their combined strengths and shared vision of "creating something from scratch and seeing it unfold," the Kayes have successfully made the transition from classroom to charter operation. With their daughter, Jennifer, they devote their working lives to introducing people to the joys of sailing and private dream-spinning on the open seas.*

KEN: For years, when someone would ask me what I did for a living, I used to say, "I teach," underline, underline, underline. But since Ellen, Jen, and I started our sail charter business, my work identity has broadened. I teach, *and* I take care of a 74-foot schooner, *and* I entertain people.

Recently I had to fill out an application, and under occupation I didn't know what to write! Sea captain? Self-employed? Business owner?

ELLEN: Sometimes I wake up and ask Ken to pinch me. Who am I? How did two people make the leap from two decades of teaching to taking people out on a schooner?

Ellen and Ken devoted a total of thirty-nine years to teaching in Connecticut school systems. While this career was a perfect fit for Ken, that wasn't the case for Ellen.

ELLEN: For years I taught art in high school. My mother had been a teacher, and even though I wanted a career as a commercial artist, I settled for teaching because in the sixties, teaching was considered a more appropriate occupation for women.

I eventually became head of the art department and set my own curriculum. But as much as I learned to enjoy teaching, I knew that there must be something better out there. Deep down I still didn't feel like I had the control I needed. No matter how hard I worked, I often felt beaten back because of the fighting we teachers had to do—for our curriculum, for our textbooks, for our supplies.

So I daydreamed all through my teaching years—about ignoring the alarm clock in the morning and not showing up for work. And of course getting away with it! It became the constant recurring theme of my life. What a reckless wish for a straight shooter like me! But since I'm also very security-oriented, I kept trudging along in my routine. I wasn't even aware that I wasn't fulfilled at work.

It was Ken's misery and search for something more satisfying that opened my eyes to my own unhappiness.

KEN: The last straw was the program cuts, which meant that I would have to teach music classes in middle school, using a curriculum that hadn't worked in the last thirty years. I would no longer have the satisfaction of teaching elementary school, where I had a band, jazz band, and orchestra.

For the first time in a long time I had to fight myself by not wishing myself sick. I felt like a failure.

ELLEN: I loved going to the faculty room every day and socializing with the other teachers. But over the years, all I heard was teachers complaining and counting the days until vacation, the days until the weekend or summer, the days until their next day off, the hours to the end of the school day. Over time I realized, My God, we're wishing our lives away.

KEN: Before the politics and program cuts finally got to me, I really loved teaching. Colleagues would actually have to remind me, "Ken, don't forget that there are only two weeks of school left." "Don't forget to pick up your paycheck." "Now, don't come in to school tomorrow, it's Saturday."

I remember this old elementary school where I actually had to teach music classes in a small room off the girls' bathroom! It had one lightbulb with no shade hanging from the ceiling. I had only one music stand that didn't work—I had to crank it up to the top of the pole to hold the music sheets. And I had ten kids huddled around the stand learning to play trumpet. Naturally, at that age they're all trying to blow their brains out while I'm counting 1, 2, 3. Invariably one of them would hit the stand, and the stand would go *chikachikachikachikachika* all the way down to the floor, and the kids would follow that music sheet down still playing their horns!

At that age kids are still independent and open to new experiences. They *want* to explore. The world is not "I will try this because my friends are." It's "I will try this because *I* want to."

ELLEN: Then by the time they're in sixth, seventh, and eighth grade, they do what everyone else does.

Likewise, Ken and Ellen knew they were headed for the same fate as their demoralized fellow teachers, counting the days to retirement. Their only hope of regaining control of their life was an honest appraisal of what they both wanted out of that life.

ELLEN: We sat down and talked about what activities we *both* loved to do. What kept coming up was the fun we had sailing our boat up to Maine every summer after the school year.

KEN: We saw so many people having a good time on their Maine Windjammer schooners. They'd drop anchor next to us and go ashore where they had built a fire on the beach. It looked like so much fun, and I remember that Ellen and I talked about what a great service that would be to provide for other people.

ELLEN: Yes, we did what a lot of people do on their summer vacation—we daydreamed about sailing for a living or going into partnership on a boat with another person. But back then it was just fantasizing.

Until Ken came up with the idea of starting a sail charter operation. I said, "Fine, but you do the initial research. If it looks good, I'm game." I wanted him to do the research instead of pushing it off on me, so that he'd have a stronger sense of ownership.

KEN: Ellen wasn't thrilled with teaching anymore, but she still had some job satisfaction and security. She told me, *"You've* got the immediate problem, not me." That remark sank in; it was a fair attitude to take.

ELLEN: We spent the whole summer before Ken's last year of teaching sailing schooners and talking to people about the business.

KEN: I also researched other, related career possibilities. I talked to a sailmaker, thinking that might be a good career change that would incorporate my love of sailing. He warned me that I would spend most of my time selling, not sailing. Then I talked to boat brokers—the general response was "You'll show a lot of boats, but not do much sailing. And you're always selling someone else's boat that you want for yourself."

ELLEN: Basically, everyone we talked to thought we were nuts, that these two burned-out teachers had lost their minds!

KEN: But then we talked to sea captains who owned their own boats, and *every* one of them said that it was a wonderful occupation with many exciting challenges.

ELLEN: By coincidence, our daughter, Jennifer, figured into the picture. While she was at college, she spent a semester crewing on a 128-foot schooner in the Caribbean.

It was a tough course—she had to take classes on board and try not to be distracted by the beautiful surroundings.

KEN: She already knew that I had to get out of this dreadful teaching situation and that we were doing research into schooner charters.

ELLEN: When she got back, she sat us down and said, "You know, you guys, *we* can do this."

Well, Ken and I were a little hesitant at first about Jen's involvement because when she went to college, we made a concentrated effort to break the ties and let her go. We felt we had made a pretty good adjustment to her leaving the nest; then suddenly we're all talking about going into business together!

Jen's coming on board was a major step, because suddenly everything started to fall into place. But at the same time it was very scary for me. We were facing a major shift in life, and I was attached to my routines: we'd always lived in Connecticut, I'd taught for x number of years. Now we had to sell the house we'd always lived in *and* the furniture, downsize all our belongings, build a boat, start up the business in Annapolis, hire a lawyer, secure capital.

To me, this dream was either going to work or not work. There was no in-between.

KEN: And all the planning in the world wouldn't guarantee success. But I had faith because both of us have always loved sailing, and I like meeting people and using my teaching skills to introduce them to the fun of sailing.

ELLEN: I look back now and I don't know how we got through those months.

KEN: It was just continuous work—we'd teach during the day, come home and gobble down our food, then do research on the charter business every night.

ELLEN: We became zombies that year, which may have been a blessing in disguise.

KEN: We were both too distracted by all the details of launching the business to let the stress get the better of us. I remember being worried about how we would get along as partners in this operation, but I think we just decided separately to put aside a lot of negative feelings.

ELLEN: I was also concerned about how Jennifer would fit into the equation now that she was an adult and living her own life.

As it turned out, we couldn't have made this business happen without her.

KEN: One of our biggest decisions was the boat itself. We wanted a boat that would provide the best sail for our customers. And we needed a custom-built schooner that would accommodate a certain number of passengers and meet rigid coast guard regulations.

ELLEN: We visited a lot of boatbuilders before we chose the one who met all our criteria for a passenger schooner. That was another big step—putting our savings into a boat.

KEN: My last day of teaching I walked out the door, hopped on a train to Albany, New York, to help build our boat, *Woodwind*. I knew nothing about boat construction, so I answered phones and watched the builders. After I'd watched for a while, they finally let me pitch in.

Everything revolved around finishing the boat as quickly as possible. It was crazy, completely different. I was so exhausted that I would fall into bed at night with my clothes on.

On the day *Woodwind* was finished, we launched her and cruised down the Hudson River. Then we took her out to sea, where we spotted a whale, came back in, and fueled up on the Chesapeake. She was cruising at 10.3 knots and it suddenly hits me that this boat is spectacular! She's so much more than just a boat. She's this incredible machine. And I'm thinking, My God, this is going to work!

Step by step, the Kayes' methodical research brought them closer to launching a new joint venture. But it wasn't an effortless transition. Even as everything fell into place, new challenges greeted them at every turn, including the change in their relationship.

ELLEN: I don't see adventure the way Ken sees adventure. He jumped into this new career with both feet. But all the upheaval was very unsettling to me.

I stayed back in Connecticut to tie up all the loose ends of our life there. And Ken headed to Annapolis to set up shop and rent an apartment. When I showed up after a few months, I was greeted by mayhem.

KEN: It's true. I had rented a tiny apartment and there were boxes everywhere. There was barely enough room to move around them. I was always on the boat, anyway, doing maintenance, training the crew. Sometimes I even slept on the boat.

ELLEN: Then I arrive and Ken says that I have to do payroll right away and take out Social Security benefits. And I'm thinking, Wait a minute. I just got here, the place is a shambles, and I've never done payroll before.

That's when the territorial battles began. I think Ken resented me showing up to help out because he felt I was trying to chip away at his control.

KEN: We had approached the entire business as a team, then I come down to Annapolis and the team dissolves for a while. When Ellen shows up, the team is supposed to come back together again. That's when the turf battles broke out and our marriage almost blew up in our faces.

ELLEN: Yeah, in two days! But we finally sat down and said to each other, "This is what you're best at, and this is what I'm best at. If we don't cross over each other's lines, we'll be fine." And it's worked ever since!

Just as they each had different strengths to contribute to their calling, Ken and Ellen also discovered that their calling gave them something in return—a separate sense of pleasure as well as the shared joy of a dream come true.

ELLEN: For me, the soul satisfaction is the variety of the business. And if Ken weren't here, I'd still do it in a blink. Ken's satisfaction is the day-to-day operation of the boat, while mine is the day-to-day operation of the business. I love figuring out what our projections are and when we will hit certain goals.

KEN: And I love making people feel comfortable, especially seeing their expressions when we set sail. Usually someone will ask, "Is the engine on?" It's incredible watching their faces light up when they discover that the boat is sailing using wind power.

ELLEN: And I feel equally excited collecting the comment cards and discovering how the business is faring!

KEN: Ellen has always been extremely creative with our finances. And I'm the exact opposite. One time I had to take a credit card payment from a passenger and I couldn't do it, so I had to ask everyone to be patient while I called Ellen to walk me through the process.

ELLEN: On those rare occasions when our transactions

don't match up, it's always on the day that Ken had his hands in the till!

You know, I discovered something about Ken *before* we went into the schooner business. He's a closet comedian! We worked that into our research—looking into what other schooners lacked in personality. We found that they weren't doing a very good job of entertaining.

That turned out to be the key to our success, and what Ken always wanted to do—entertain people and have fun. And now that's the biggest compliment we get from the passengers—Ken's personality!

KEN: Being a musician, I naturally want to entertain. Now I can sing and tell stories for my own amusement and the amusement of our passengers.

ELLEN: We're both healthier, too. When I was teaching I had a lot of physical problems—gum disease, colds. Since I quit, I haven't had a single cold and my gum disease disappeared.

Plus my dream came true about sleeping through the alarm clock. Now I wake up naturally and feel full of energy.

Really, Ken and I have been very lucky. It's like there's a golden cloud hanging over us. What we set out to do, we achieve. It's like the roadblocks aren't even there anymore.

KEN: Nothing pleases me more than people remembering what a wonderful experience they had on our schooner. And in the years to come what a wonderful business this is for our future grandchildren to enjoy. Whether *Woodwind* stays in our family or not, she's too fine a boat not to have a long life bringing pleasure to others.

ELLEN: Every time we set sail, there are forty-some passengers on *Woodwind* for a couple of hours. And in that space of time, each one of them is in his or her own little world.

One of our frequent passengers is a high-powered lawyer from Washington, D.C. He always leaves a fifty-dollar tip. One day I finally asked him, "I know the money is not an issue for you, but why do you leave such a generous tip?" And he said, "These are the only two hours I can spend, just to myself, without interruption."

That taught me something about what our business means to others. It's more than just a pleasant sail on the Chesapeake. You don't choose a boat to go quickly from point A to point B. People use *Woodwind* as a key to unlock their daydreams, their fantasies.

8

Look to Your Family for Strength

If you don't have any understanding of who you are or what you're about, then you cannot be of benefit or help to yourself or others.

MARY JANE KOLAR

55, CEO and Turnaround Specialist

What we learn at our family's knee—whether good or bad—wields a powerful influence over how we view ourselves and our place in the world. Do we prize physical strength or strength of character? Are we moved to action by passionate displays of emotion or by introspective self-analysis? Do we prefer comedy over drama? Teamwork over going it alone?

How we think, how we act, how we work, and even

how we play are rooted in family—that first human mirror reflecting back to us who we are and who we may some-day be. And long after we leave the nest, to make our own way in the world, our family stays locked inside us, contin-uing to influence the choices we make.

CEO Mary Jane Kolar is a transitional leader. Her directive: to reengineer, invigorate, inspire . . . then leave. With five different or-ganizations she has provided the vision and leadership needed to de-velop their ability to turn themselves around.

Her nearly three decades of experience in the field of professional association management have earned her numerous awards and the highest respect of the people who have worked for her. Everything about her—her tailored suits, her impeccable manners, her direct eye contact—suggests an upbringing filled with unlimited educational, social, and professional opportunities.

But looks can be deceiving. You see, Mary Jane grew up in a southern Illinois coal-mining town where there were no special privi-leges. Instead she had something far more valuable—the love and in-fluence of her parents, two fiercely independent and strong-willed individuals who had high expectations for themselves and their daughters.

Years later, Mary Jane still puts into practice what they taught her so very long ago—that the most important thing in life is human potential, and you can't help others realize theirs if you don't live up to your own.

My father once said that he hoped I never got the coal dust completely out from underneath my fingernails. He was right—we're much more influenced by our roots than we think. And we're more reliant on others than we'd like to believe. You don't become successful on your own.

I learned that lesson early on when I ran away from home at fifteen and married the local football hero. In those days married girls were encouraged to leave school. Both my parents and my home economics teacher came to my defense, convincing the school that it would be a waste of human potential for me not to graduate. Mom and Dad also insisted I receive the scholarship I had earned so that I could start college the summer after my graduation.

Certainly my parents were driving forces in my life! My father was a coal miner and my mother was a teacher. They were thirty-two and thirty-seven when I was born, and I was their first child.

I was a reasonably good child but strong-minded—my parents fostered that. They always encouraged my sister and me to speak our minds, to develop our own sense of self—probably unique for young women growing up in the 1950s.

Education was highly prized by both of Mary Jane's parents, and they taught her the value of ideas and open discussion. They never set any limits on learning because they knew from their own experience that, without a good education, it would be an uphill struggle for their daughters to reach their full potential.

My father, one of eleven children, was an unusual man for his time and occupation. He thought that an education was the best insurance policy anyone could have. He himself had run away from home at fifteen and lied about his age to join the army in World War I. Later, he finished high school, but he had already started a family and never went beyond the twelfth grade.

When he and my mother married in 1929, he encouraged her to get her baccalaureate degree despite the fact that during the Depression married women weren't allowed to teach—those jobs were for men who supported families!

My mother was one of nine children and the only one to go beyond high school. After twenty years of teaching, she became a high school guidance counselor. I remember her distress when she learned that men in the counseling department were making more money than women, and of course the explanation she was given was that men had families to feed.

I come from a long line of strong women! My great-grandmother wildcatted oil wells in Texas. My grandmother, whose older husband died and left her with two small children, was extremely industrious, always doing something to make ends meet. I remember going to her house, sitting by the stove to stay warm, and helping to cut out quilt blocks. Women of her era just didn't have time to feel sorry for themselves.

I grew up in a home where the mother always worked—one of the few in town who did—but that didn't seem strange to me. My mother's in her eighties now and still very active. To tell you the truth, I still don't think I'd want to go head-to-head with her! She's a very formidable person.

Mary Jane grew up in an era when for most Americans there were no long, self-indulgent discussions about which career to pursue or what college to attend. The talk, especially in a coal-mining town, was of getting a job and putting food on the table.

Life wasn't exactly sensitive to the individual back then. A lot of men who came home from the Second World War had families they needed to support, so many of them worked in the coal mines. Most of the men in my town didn't live to an old age; even today there are very few older men.

But that's the environment I knew. And it still affects me today. I remember when one of my uncles was killed in a mining accident. Whenever there was an accident, the mine whistle would blow. Everyone in town knew what it meant and rushed to their porches. I always ran into my room and huddled in the corner with my arms covering my head, for fear that someone close to me had been injured. To this day I can't hear a loud mine-like whistle without it taking me back to the stark reality of those days.

Once I became a teen, I went through a phase all teenagers go through—I thought my parents didn't want me to do the things that other kids did. My father was always arriving to drive me home from an activity before I was ready to leave, and for an adolescent that's very embarrassing. On top of it, I was rather intellectual and a bit of an ugly duckling. I was only fifteen when I was a senior in high school. In those days the school system wasn't prepared to deal with highly motivated students except to double- and triple-promote them, which certainly presents challenges in the area of social adjustment.

So what do I do to rebel? I leave home the same age my father did! But when you're married that young, you look around and there just aren't many options. On the other hand, I'm not sure there would have been any more options in that tiny town even if I hadn't been married. The choices were pretty narrow for women in 1958. Teaching seemed the only solution. It took me five years to earn a baccalaureate degree, and during that time I had two children. However, I did begin to teach in a three-room country school in 1960 where I had fifty-six preparations every day. That experience actually helped me to be able to handle almost anything.

A lot of people in town thought I should quit teaching, stop going to college, and stay at home. But I was convinced I needed an education and a job! Maybe those involvements were a way out of an unsuccessful marriage and on some level I understood that.

Teaching also may have been another way of earning my parents' recognition. It's not that they weren't proud of my accomplishments, but they were like a lot of other parents—they told everyone else how proud they were but never told me!

Without realizing it, Mary Jane was developing the skills she would rely on as a teacher and a turnaround specialist. Like her parents, she began to look within herself for guidance, using what she had learned to turn her own life around.

I remember in 1963 receiving a telegram from my university saying that I was going to receive the Phi Beta Kappa commencement prize and graduate number one in my class. I suddenly realized, as I sat down on the curb with the piece of paper in my hand, that I had accomplished a great deal more than I had expected to and was very proud that I hadn't let everyone down who had believed in me and my ability to succeed.

That was a breakthrough for me. I decided that I would stop focusing as much on earning the approval of others. It's not that I didn't care about what others thought. It was just that I began to question how well others could really evaluate me. Perhaps they could evaluate the results of my efforts, but not me as a person; only I could do that. And many people don't come to that understanding until very late in life.

After ten years of teaching in Illinois public schools, Mary Jane went on to a second career in association management, where she found that although the environment had changed, the lesson was still the same.

Whether teaching or running an organization, the hardest lesson I've had to learn over the years is that people can only move so quickly. I have to fight the urge to jump in and try to change everything right away.

But as a CEO for organizations in transition, I'm there to help turn the organization around, to revitalize it. And that meant that I sometimes have to make difficult staffing decisions affecting people's lives. When that was necessary, I would try to act on a Monday. Most people are terminated on Fridays, which I think is a mistake. That means they have an entire weekend to feel terrible about what's happened to them. But if you lose your job at the beginning of the week, you have to decide what to do next right away as well as move forward with your job search.

The truth is, if an organization is to survive and thrive in the future—which ultimately translates into employment for a good number of people—then I have had to take strong actions and sometimes make difficult decisions immediately.

It hasn't always made me popular, but I can go home at night and look at myself in the mirror, believing that not only have I done the right thing, but ultimately I've saved more jobs than I've had to sacrifice.

The work I do is very satisfying to me, almost an elixir. It is often so all-consuming that when it's time to leave, I always have mixed feelings after working so intensely on the turnaround effort. But my fundamental value as a leader within organizations in transition is to teach the organization to set new goals and stay focused on achieving those goals based on shared values. Once that's accomplished, I'm a pull-down-the-window-shade type—my work is finished and it's time to move on.

I think my father was also a pull-down-the-window-shade person as well. I remember distinctly the in-depth discussions we had before he died. He told me that he had accomplished all he wanted to do in his life. As a result, when he died, at sixty, he was at peace, he had no real regrets.

And that's the way I've tried to live my life too—free of guilt and free of regrets. My father's death was traumatic for me and my family. But I believe that once you've faced difficult life experiences head on, you realize that you can deal with whatever an action-oriented life brings.

That's why I think that one of the best things that can happen to everyone is to have to go through career changes and upheavals, because only then do you discover that challenges are something you *can* deal with and move on from. It's actually a part of the process of living!

Life isn't out *there* somewhere; it's inside you. And if you don't have any understanding of who you are and what you're about, then you cannot be of benefit or help to yourself or others.

9

Know That Support Surrounds You

As I look on my own life, every time something
bad happened, something good came out of it. I finally
understand how I got to this point and
why I'm on this earth.

JAMES HARDEMAN

53, Head of Employee Assistance Program, Polaroid Corporation

While your calling may be unique to you, that doesn't mean you have to do it alone. Help will come from just about anyone anywhere, both expected and unexpected. Your family. Your God. Your employer. The person sitting next to you on a plane.

Everyone needs support along the way; it's that helping hand we give to one another that makes great things happen in this world.

Once you realize that there are others who share your vision and are just as committed as you are to turning that dream into a reality, the right doors will open, one by one.

Running the employee assistance program of one of the country's largest corporations could be quite the power trip. After all, the health and productivity of the company is inexorably tied to the health and productivity of its employees. Who has a finger on the company's pulse more than the EAP department?

For Jim Hardeman, health and productivity are the natural outcomes of finding and living your calling. And he applies that same principle to himself. Polaroid has been a supportive platform from which Jim could pursue his own calling—to stop the rampant and ugly abuse that is tearing apart so many American families.

Jim is a product of that abuse. Yet there's a warmth and compassion to his demeanor that belies his past. He will tell you unabashedly that his life has been marked by miracles. More to the point, he's certain he's on this earth for a reason, and right now he's at Polaroid because that's where God wants him to be. That's the message he conveys to everyone in his life, including Polaroid and its employees.

Case in point: When Polaroid announced it was downsizing— resulting in thousands of lost jobs—all department heads had to make a presentation before the CEO explaining why their individual departments should not be dismantled.

Jim was already losing some of his employees, but his entire department—that possibility would be enough to send most supervisors into nail-biting paranoia. Not Jim. He immediately set about guiding his staff to see beyond the present situation and understand that the knowledge and skills they had to offer the world would find a new home. Sound naive?

Not at all. When you're following your calling, like Jim, the support is always there.

Many of Polaroid's employees come to me for spiritual counseling. I tell them that they have so many talents that can be used elsewhere; Polaroid doesn't have to be the end-all. Those who are leaving the company, I tell them that they are more valuable now than when they started at Polaroid, that they're truly blessed. As soon as their names get out there—after all they've learned here—they'll see what I mean.

Whenever bad things happen, I now ask myself, What are the opportunities? I may not see them right away, but I'm going to hang tight and eventually they'll be revealed.

With my faith, I'm never alone. It's given me such confidence in dealing with troubled times that I no longer self-destruct. Without God and the support He sends, I couldn't do any of the things I'm doing right now.

As I look on my own life, every time something bad happened, something good came out of it. I finally understand how I got to this point and why I'm on this earth.

Jim's strong inner core of understanding was forged by violence at a tender age, at a time when a child desperately needs to be loved and accepted.

I grew up with fifteen years of child abuse. My father had his own strange way of discipline. It started when I was eight years old, when my father tied my hands and feet behind me—hog-tied me—and hung me from the ceiling. He used a stick to beat me, like I was a piñata.

My mother couldn't stop him. She had to run and get the neighbors. At eight years old, I had to wonder what I could have done that would make him do something horrible like that to me. And there was never any explanation.

So I turned the abuse into a game, a contest: you'll never see me cry. After a while it was as though someone had given me Novocain throughout my entire body. One punch was like the hundredth punch. And I felt like I was winning. He would be sweating and tired from hitting me, and I would walk away without shedding a tear and think, I've won.

The way my mother dealt with it, since she couldn't physically stop it, was to line up her children on the bed and read the Bible. The whole time my mother was praying and talking to God, I would be looking for God. Since I was the oldest and spokesperson for my brothers and sisters, I would ask, "Where is He? I don't see Him. If your God doesn't show up soon and stop this maniac, I'm not praying anymore."

And she would just say to me, "Someday." That's what we kids would walk away with, that Mom said, "Someday." She never finished the sentence.

I didn't understand what she meant until just a few years ago. She meant that someday I'd be out of this situation— she didn't know when, but she knew. Someday this tragedy would end and I could move on with my life.

Jim was never angry with his mother for not protecting him or his siblings from harm. She gave out so much love and support that it helped to counterbalance the evil deeds of his father. "She was doing her best," he says, "and my father was doing his worst." This marked the start of turning toward the good in his life and not letting himself be swallowed up by the bad.

Because of the beatings, I had to get out of the house. And that's when I joined the Boy Scouts. For the first time in my life there were men who explained things to me. We went camping and I learned about the outdoors; to this day being outdoors means everything to me. I felt safer in the woods than at home, and I learned a sense of peace.

In seventh and eighth grades, I was in the "dummy

class." Yet the teachers passed me. They gave me words of encouragement, telling me I was going to make something of myself. One teacher told me I was a gentleman and a scholar. And by the end of ninth grade, I was an honor student. I had developed an outlook of positivism. Even though home was bad, school was good.

In high school I was on the track team and could run and run and not remember anything, like I was running unconsciously. I could put myself in another world. Even now when I go to the dentist, I don't need painkillers because nothing hurts when I'm in my other world.

One of my greatest desires was to go to West Point. Those guys looked so sharp in their uniforms. My guidance counselor told me I would never measure up. But my paper route customers encouraged me. In fact, a lady on the route drove me to the entrance exam for West Point. I failed the first time, but when I took it again my freshman year of college, I passed. (I decided not to go since I had already been through the first year of college, but passing the test made me feel good, especially since they sent the notice to my high school guidance counselor!)

When Jim left home for college, he was all alone with no money. But along the way, people continued to offer him their support, something Jim still found perplexing.

I went to Howard University with no tuition money, no

money at all. I wasn't afraid, because in my mind I was leaving all that behind. When you have to fight and you're getting collared all the time, the unknown is easy.

For the first three months I ate one meal a day —a hamburger and french fries—until I could figure out how I could make it. I worked as a busboy and people trusted me, so they gave me loans for school. I was a C student, but other students making A's and B's still wanted to study with me. People saw things in me that I didn't see.

This was also during the civil rights movement and I was so angry with white people making judgments based on skin color. I thought, Here we go again, God. I'm a black man, I've got child abuse at home, and now I have to deal with an abusive society. I'm just plain fucked. When is it going to be my turn?

There was to be no immediate answer to Jim's question. After graduating, he moved to Massachusetts, where he continued his graduate studies in social work, working nights at a community mental health center. What happened next catapulted Jim into his calling.

One night a woman with a baby came to the door and said her husband was beating her and she needed shelter. I told her that the center wasn't a shelter; we only did counseling. I didn't have any clothing for her baby, nothing. Her response to me was "Now I know why my husband didn't chase me. He knew I would have to return."

A week later I read about the same woman in the newspaper. Her husband beat her in broad daylight on the steps of the post office! How could anyone stand by and let this happen? He was never arrested, and she was taken to the nearest shelter, forty-five minutes away.

I was so shaken I went to my boss and said, "The next time a woman comes here for shelter, the next morning you're going to find a family living here." He told me that if it bothered me so much, I should do something about it. He put the challenge out to me. So at the next staff meeting, I asked for all of the cases dealing with spouse abuse. I started a battered women's group with one of my interns as the co-therapist.

I didn't know it, but within a year's time, I would have a battered women's shelter. I went to a doctor and a nurse at the emergency room for their help. I went to the courts for help. I went to all the key people and put them on my board of directors for the shelter. They all said yes to me.

The only ones who said no were the clergy. They thought either the problem didn't exist or they would know about it first. I told them that they would be the last to know because victims of domestic violence keep it a secret.

The battered women in my group couldn't afford an attorney because their husbands were controlling the purse strings. So we made the group sessions part clinical and part educational, including in-services with lawyers. The women began to represent themselves and were winning, even when their husbands had attorneys.

The National Organization for Women heard about this and asked me to do speaking engagements in the area. They set up meetings where I would talk about domestic violence, then pass the hat and give me the money for the shelter.

That got us a hot line. Then I asked for a grant from the Comprehensive Employment and Training Act (CETA), and the woman I submitted it to said, "Even though we've just met for the first time, you can count on getting the money." She said she had been a battered woman and had no shelter available to her. The money I got from CETA I used to rent a house for the shelter. It finally began to dawn on me that this was meant to be.

Word got out in the community about the shelter, the court cases, my talks; soon the newspapers began covering me and my work. One by one, women showed up and asked if they could work for me, even if I couldn't pay them. They became my original staff when we opened the shelter doors.

This was a miracle! We had a shelter in twelve months servicing thirteen families. After a few months, I turned it over to the staff. I just wanted to get it started; I never wanted to own it or run it. To this day, my role is to raise money for the shelter, not to hold office.

It's something that I promised myself, that I would never accept money from speaking on this issue; I would always give it away.

Jim says that his hatred toward his father and his desire to kill him were so strong, he often thought he might very well end up behind bars. He was also terrified that he himself might become a batterer.

I was so grateful that I hadn't ended up in prison. But after all these years, I still hadn't talked to anyone about my own child abuse! At forty I began having nightmares about it and would wake up screaming. When you're a victim of child abuse, you grow up with no one to explain things to you. You have a mind full of questions, and there is no significant other, no mentor, no one you can go to and say, "Explain, explain." I had so much garbage in my head that I wanted to put it all out on the table.

I went into therapy, and it took six years before I realized that someone was looking over my shoulder every step of my life. I had so much rage, I could've killed, but I wasn't a batterer. Instead, God was there, leading me.

And sending me support. When I was accepted at Harvard to attend the master's program, I was married with two kids, so I had to work. But when the dean found out I was working, he told me I wouldn't make it through the program. He even pulled out his slide rule to measure my success and said it showed that I wouldn't make it! I told him right then that he had no idea how hard I'd worked to get here and I would never let this opportunity go by.

It turned out that the dean's secretary overheard his comments and told me later that she would do any typing I needed. She was the first person I looked up to at Harvard. The second person was the librarian, who would sneak out the books I needed at closing, which I couldn't check out during the day because of my job. I would return them early the next morning before the library opened so she wouldn't get in trouble.

I didn't attend my graduation. The real people who gave me my graduation were the secretary and the librarian; we had our own celebration of three!

Jim went to work for Governor Michael Dukakis in the state's human services department. But a failed marriage and discrimination at work sent his life into a tailspin.

When I filed for divorce, it was a major loss. I never had family growing up and it was what I always wanted. I thought I'd found it when I married and had kids. But I was wrong. I became very depressed and almost collapsed at work.

The woman who helped me get my CETA grant was now working in the statehouse as a secretary. She went to my boss and said she was worried about me.

During this time I had friends at work who were being fired because they were Republican. Even though my job performance was perfect, my employers began putting pressure on me, telling me that I wasn't part of the team anymore because I had the wrong friends! Because of my friends I was being punished. No one touches my friends; they're golden to me.

I was isolated from key meetings. I went to the governor and told him what was going on; he sent a letter telling my department to lay off. That made them even more furious and every day a total hell for me, so I resigned.

The despair Jim felt over his divorce and unemployment was about to be eased by individuals extending a hand to him—people he didn't even know.

I went from priest to priest about my failed marriage, but they all said that I shouldn't get divorced, that it was against the church. One day I went to confession, and the priest asked me if I felt like a good person. "If you do," he said, "then you should leave the confessional and do what you need to do." At last God had sent me someone who related to me as a person, not as the church.

At an alumni meeting I talked about the circumstances surrounding my resignation, and afterward someone must have sent my name in to Polaroid. To this day I don't know who. Polaroid called me and, bingo, I was hired to head up the employee assistance program at one of Polaroid's six sites. God comes through again. I'm beginning to get the message.

One day an employee at Polaroid was met by her boss in the lobby. He pointed at his watch and said, "Late again." She began screaming and collapsed. He was shocked by her reaction and suggested that they both go to the counseling department. I talked with them and found out that she was a victim of spouse abuse and that she knew other women at Polaroid who were being beaten. I asked her if they would come forward, and one by one they came to my office, from the assembly line up to management. From that we started the first battered women's group in a company.

Word leaked out about the group. The head of internal communications asked me if she could film the women's stories. I didn't let on that it was a group for battered women and asked the group what they wanted to do.

They had already talked among themselves and wanted to share their stories of abuse. So the film was made and shown at Polaroid's next business meeting.

Years later the head of internal communications became assistant to the president of the company. She called me and said there was a vacancy to head Polaroid's entire EAP, and she wanted me because she liked the way I ran my individual site like a business, not just a counseling operation.

Once I became head of Polaroid's employee assistance program, incredible things began to happen. I was able to run a battered women's shelter from inside a corporation. I sat on the board of the Polaroid Foundation. I had the foundation members visit shelters near Polaroid's manufacturing plants so they could see for themselves how Polaroid employees had to go there after work. After that, they pledged their yearly support.

Then the Battered Women's Coalition of Massachusetts asked me to meet with them to start a Jane Doe Safety Fund because all the shelters in the state were full and they had to turn women away. They needed a flagship donor, and I said there was only one corporation in America for that role and that was Polaroid. Polaroid wrote a check for $75,000—the largest single grant ever given in the sixty-three years of the corporation. Within eleven months that check for $75,000 turned into $1 million. (I've always been able to make money happen because I give it away; it doesn't own me.) Once again, it was God working through me.

Jim moves with the grace of a man who is fully engaged in his life's purpose. His next step: the creation of a national summit on domestic violence and child abuse. Planning an event of this size and scope would be overwhelming for most of us, but Jim has already enlisted the help of major companies and organizations, including the White House.

He has learned his lesson well: Support for your calling is always there, sometimes even when you don't ask for it.

So much has been revealed to me about my life: I'm alive; I'm not a batterer; I have a close relationship with my kids. And then getting a phone call from the White House to meet the president because of my work with battered women!

When I met with President Clinton, I invited him to be the keynote speaker at the national summit I'm planning. It will be a gathering of organizations directly and indirectly involved with battered women and children who are sexually assaulted. Right now there are model programs in this country that work, but each state doesn't know what all of the others are doing.

We're going to fix that. We'll identify the top programs

in each category dealing with battered women—for example, emergency medical treatment, insurance, the courts, social services, research, funding. Then we're going to fly in to Boston the movers and shakers from each program, plus the executive director of the battered women's coalition in each state.

The marching orders will be: Leave your title and how much money you make at the door and be ready to roll up your sleeves. You're going to come up with a bible of model programs that people can take back to their states.

From this summit we're also going to create a curriculum for kindergarten through high school dealing with issues of dating violence, family violence, and child abuse. Every school system in America will teach the same curriculum.

The money will come for this, I know it! And now when things like this happen I know that God is orchestrating everything in my life. I will look for these opportunities, and I know what He wants me to do. And I know what my mother meant. Someday. And someday is right now. Life has come full circle. All the adversity in my life was a prelude to what I'm supposed to be doing now.

Someday all the specialists in domestic violence will come together and form our own institute. We're going to change the face of the world.

10

Engage Both
Your Head and
Your Heart

*Your heart is your motivator. The challenge is to come
up with the solutions that will resolve the problem. And
that sometimes requires untraditional thinking.*

MARC PAULHUS

43, Animal Cruelty Investigator

There may come a time when you observe another's agony
so powerful that you feel it keenly in your own bones. This
injustice will haunt your empathic heart and ultimately
drive you to marshal all your abilities and knowledge to
end this suffering. From that moment forward it will be
your calling to fight against this pain, to witness it unblink-
ingly and report it back to the rest of the world.

This is a calling only for the strong. It will require more

patience, more stamina, and more courage than you ever imagined you had. It will also give you the patience, the stamina, and the courage you need to fight the good fight.

But you will need one more arrow in your quiver: a cool head. Temper your passion with a calm, creative, and strategic mind. You'll be amazed how easy it is to outwit your opponent. And from time to time, it might even keep you alive. That's the ultimate staying power.

It's entirely possible that Marc Paulhus owes his life to the fact that ten strangers were mysteriously compelled to lie to their friends about him. He was working undercover investigating a dogfighting ring of about 250 people, and a corrupt sheriff tipped off the leader that undercover operatives would be witnessing the next event. Dogfighting is a cruel, bloody sport that breeds and trains dogs to rip each other apart—often to the death. This is a secret society of abuse, drugs, gambling, and prostitution. As dedicated as Marc was to breaking this vicious sport, its participants were equally dedicated to protecting this way of life.

At that particular moment, however, the most important difference was that Marc and his partner were outnumbered by hundreds of "good dog men"—who had guns.

The owner of the property got in the middle of the pit

and announced, "We have some informants here. Everybody must stand up and be identified by at least two other
people as good dog men that you've known for a long
time." I knew no one in the room except for my partner
and our informant for more than twenty-four hours. And
that was only because I had played poker with them the
night before.

At least ten people stood up in the room and verified
me. I have no idea why it happened, but it saved my butt.
And I know firsthand what that expression about being
scared means. I had diarrhea for days later.

In retrospect I don't think I was in danger of my life if I
had been caught. But I think the informant who brought us
in could have been killed. Would have? I don't know. But
definitely could have.

*While a cool head from time to time protected Marc and his mis-
sion, more often a creative approach would save his day. As it did
the night events transformed his simple, just-for-now livelihood into
his life's work.*

I grew up in Connecticut wanting to be a veterinarian,
but the competition for admission was too stiff at Cornell
(the region's only veterinary school at the time). So after
graduating from the University of Connecticut, I moved to
Florida, where a new school was due to be opened in a

couple of years. I figured that would give me time to work on my master's degree and establish residency.

I looked for an animal-related job there because I thought the experience would help with my vet school admission later. So I went to the St. Petersburg SPCA. I'd had only had a little shelter experience in Connecticut when I worked as a part-time animal control officer. But that was more or less because I had dated the police chief's daughter in high school and the shelter was under him. But I had enjoyed it, so it seemed the St. Petersburg SPCA was as good a place as any to start looking for a job.

I just showed up and asked what was available. By coincidence it needed a nighttime ambulance driver, a position that provided housing on the property. So supposedly my days were free to go to school.

Something about that work set me on fire. I got so absolutely absorbed in the job I was like a twenty-four-hour employee. If I had free time, I would assist with surgery. Saturdays and Sundays were my days off, but since I lived on the property I would go to work anyway. It was an absolute obsession, and I was deliriously happy. It felt like I was doing something valuable and significant and was appreciated by the community—even though the financial rewards were absolutely zip. I was one of the good guys.

Marc remembers one case in particular that was the flint for the kindling: When at 3:00 A.M. he found himself with a goat and a stack of law books, trying to figure out how to get the maximum punishment for a couple of men found on the beach nearby. The condition of the goat could have distracted him from his mission, but his intellect kicked into gear and his creativity brought him the solution that changed his life.

The St. Petersburg Beach Police had just arrested these guys for having sex with the goat on the beach. They had cut its throat so it couldn't bleat and it was breathing out of the hole in its trachea.

The police didn't know what to do or what to charge these guys with. They had never had a case of animal cruelty, and the SPCA didn't have a cruelty investigator. I spent the next two or three hours in the police chief's office and found that cruelty statutes were only minor misdemeanors and carried only a maximum fine of $1,000 or six months in jail.

But then I found one of those really archaic statutes that were passed in the 1890s when people talked of sex in obtuse terms. It was basically an antisodomy statute, and the title of it was Crimes Against Nature, stating that committing lewd and lascivious acts in violation of the natural order is a felony of the third degree.

No one had ever applied that statute to anything before.

One guy got nine years and the other guy got eight years. (Since the statute called for only five years, the fact that they had been on probation already and were found with marijuana increased their sentence.)

Your heart is your motivator. The challenge is to come up with the solutions that will resolve the problem. And that sometimes requires untraditional thinking.

That was the case that started the animal abuse investigation program at the St. Petersburg SPCA. I got a lot of press, and we went from zero cases to three hundred a year. I was very emotionally up. It was a personal mission, a very intense thing. I had found something I never thought I could find. It was a hell of a realization to discover that I had lucked into a job that suited me totally.

This growing role was also Marc's catalyst for defining for himself what humane treatment is, and his own relationship to animals.

I didn't have a philosophy or an emerging ethic that said all animals suffer and should be humanely treated. Basically the training I had in college animal husbandry courses fostered the utilitarian approach to animals. That they're to be treated as humanely as is necessary to promote growth and economic viability. College had deadened my feelings toward animals.

The goat episode angered me but it was still a job. I was doing the things that mechanically needed to be done. But

I had a sense of outrage. Why? It was unusual. These guys were sick and twisted.

The unusual was really shocking. But I was desensitized to the usual. The St. Petersburg shelter at the time was filled with neglected, skinny, and mange-ridden animals. Between the years 1975 and 1977 I probably helped euthanize between 5,000 and 6,000 animals, at least.

But there are some animals I still remember. One dog I picked up wasn't a cruelty case per se. It had been hit by a car and dragged. It was literally skinned alive. That dog was so sweet that even though it was in so much pain it didn't try to bite me. The dogs you pick up on the highway invariably try to bite you because they don't know you don't want to cause them any more pain. You want to handle them gently, but you can't, even if you put them on a stretcher. And I had to carry them in my arms because I had no assistant with me in the middle of the night.

I should have put that dog to sleep that night. But that dog just adored me, and let me put the skin back on her without biting me. The vet came in the next morning and said, "Marc why did you let that dog live?" I could only answer, "Because she wants to live. Can't we save her?"

The two of us put in over three hundred stitches—I remember the vet calling them mattress stitches. I fed and cared for the animal for weeks and weeks. And finally put her up for adoption. But no one wanted her because she was an ugly dog.

After four months of being in a cage, she was finally put to sleep. That killed me. Still does.

I couldn't adopt her myself because I already had two dogs and a cat. This wasn't a healthy place to have pets because there were diseased animals I came into contact every day. I was fighting the urge all the time to adopt every cruelty case that I had. It's an occupational hazard; every animal has a story.

While Marc's early court case brought him renown—and an increased workload—he quickly discovered that court was the last resort. And he developed new skills of cooperation toward change.

I had people pull guns on me, so I would just go back later and start to wear them down. And most of the time it worked. Because I had no legal authority and didn't carry a gun, I was fairly unthreatening. So I learned to put my effort in the front end and say, "Hi, I'm Marc Paulhus, and I'm with the SPCA and guess what. I've got a complaint I have to work on and I'm here to work with you, not against you."

But every once in a while I would get someone who flunked the attitude test, the kind who would pull out a gun and say, "Get the hell off my property." Only then would I take the tough approach and come back with the police.

His work soon came to the attention of the Humane Society of the United States, a Washington-based humane organization that hired him away from his Florida home and thrust him into two new worlds: state- and national-level lobbying and undercover work.

Legislative work was an intellectual challenge. I had no training, so I had to develop my own approach to it. The moral argument has such an advantage over weak, selfish arguments. You don't have to buy people. You don't have to wine and dine.

You have to be willing to compromise. You can't expect to get everything you want, and you can never lie. What we're trading in is trust, justice, compassion, all those Boy Scout virtues. I have a philosophy that's consistent; if it's not in accordance with everybody else's, at least it's consistent. And I have to be prepared to defend myself because that's often part of the legislative agenda.

I'm not the answer to the world. I'm a technician. I know how to get the job done, and I think I'm doing some things that are good. In this business you can only stay on fire if you think you are being effective, and you can only be effective if you're not in personal conflict.

But the other part of his work did put him in that personal conflict. He would spend weeks and months infiltrating dogfighting rings, betraying his deepest values and principles. These were days when he chummed with men whose best joy is watching the bloody battles of vicious dogs. Throats are torn out, and blood and saliva fly as the dogs lunge at each other. At the end, the loser is often summarily shot in the head. Sometimes the winner also. With no official police authority, Marc and his Humane Society of the United States partners could only work with local law enforcement—hoping that the police were not corrupt as well.

Dogfighters are a rough crowd. In order to do this work you have to enter into a new role. You have to define for yourself someone who is not disgusted by dogfighting, but who is really into it. You have to cheer when you really want to wince. You can't betray your feelings.

I would dedicate about three or four months of under-cover work before a series of busts would start taking place. You have to be convincing to infiltrate that deeply for that long. But what was most difficult for me was coming out of that role when my work was done.

When I came back into my ordinary life, my vocabulary was still gutter vocabulary, and I had an overly forceful way of dealing with people in the office. Not abusive, really, but definitely in-your-face.

It's similar to the problem cops have working with lowlifes on the street. They've got to show an edge that says, "If this is going to turn violent, I'm ready, buddy." It's posturing more than anything. But it's very difficult to turn off and on and off and on.

I was delighted when I moved out of dogfighting to deal with abusers who were less on the edge.

Today Marc is the HSUS's director of equine protection. His focus now is on the treatment of horses, from the personal horse in someone's backyard to the training of Tennessee walking horses to the famous wild pony roundup on Chincoteague Island to the folly of the brutal three-day events under the Atlanta heat during the 1996 Olympics.

It is a never-ending sequence of abusive conditions that must be resolved. Still, it is the isolated moment now and then that shimmers in Marc's mind, that renews his sensitivity to the poignant suffering of animals and that motivates him to continue.

There was a Tennessee–walking horse trainer who returned a horse to a client in terrible shape. He was 400 to 500 pounds underweight, his testicles were three times their normal size, he had contracted tendons, and there were signs of deliberate soring around the horse's feet. So I went to visit the man. With the local police.

He was initially very belligerent and threatened to shoot us if we didn't leave. After the police talked him down, I discovered about twenty horses still at the farm. You could see shadows behind their ribs and their hip cages were prominent. In the back pasture I found the carcasses of seventeen dead horses, mostly picked clean by vultures. There was also an abandoned house that he had been using as a barn. One of the bedrooms in the house had been used as a stall, but the floor had caved in, and the decomposed body of a horse was found in the cellar.

It was toward the end of my initial investigation that I noticed a big white emaciated dog trotting across the field, disappearing down an embankment next to a creek. She was carrying something in her mouth. When I followed her I saw it was a dead puppy that she had in her mouth.

What she was doing was taking her dead puppy to the creek to bury it. She dug a hole, put the puppy in the hole, pushed dirt over the puppy with her nose, and then sat there for a long time. Goose bumps flashed through me. It was obvious she was aware of a tragedy that had just occurred.

To my knowledge animals don't bury their dead. They mourn them, certainly, and dogs have been known to stay with their dead an hour or so. But this was just so extraordinary and eerie.

There have been a lot of different moments that have been scary. I've had victories and losses in my career. But in terms of poignancy and a recurring sad image, nothing affects me more than that. A singular dog in that one incident. I've seen much worse things. But this one just stays with me.

It takes enduring strength to continue with this work, to be sure. It also takes strength to resist the temptation to indict all of humanity when our species is so capable of committing unspeakable cruelties. To the contrary, Marc says that his work not only relieves the suffering of animals, it also breaks the cycle of abuse that can extend to other helpless creatures—children, for example.

Animal cruelty is an indicator crime. If someone can so lose his temper to cause serious injury because the dog peed on the carpet, that person can also put his wife in the hospital emergency room because she burned the dinner. Those who actively abuse animals tend to abuse people.

My work puts me in touch with the worst of people. But it also takes me to the best of people, whose compassion is so boundless that it doesn't just extend to their family, their friends, or other members of their species. But it extends to animals, too.

One of the biggest fallacies I've encountered is that people will say of someone, "He loves animals but doesn't love human beings." That's impossible. Everyone I know who is engaged in humane work is also engaged in human rights issues or other struggles involving suffering and compassion.

Kindness and compassion are not species-specific. You are either kind or you're not. You're either compassionate or you're not.

11

Hold Out for the Best

*You can go either high-end or mediocre. Don't sell
yourself short. Go with what your heart tells you to do,
even if it means you have to wait a while longer.*

SUZANNE DUNLAP

30, Hairstylist

A calling requires high-quality outlets for its expression.
You deserve to work with people who respect you and
treat you kindly. And you should only work for companies
that take pride in the excellence of their products. However, society has bought into the myth of limited opportunities. So you might be tempted to take any job in your
field that comes your way, perhaps settling for a company
with mediocre standards, or being with the wrong group

of people who can't appreciate the true value of the gifts you bring to your work.

Sure, there are dues to pay. And beginners must start where they can. But you are about important work. Your calling is your first-class ticket to the world. Don't compromise your mission by submitting to shabby treatment or standards.

Suzanne Dunlap works in perhaps the finest hair salon in town. Suzanne's station is nearest the big front window of the quaint Colonial-era row house that has been fitted out with sinks and mirrors. She picked that spot so she could enjoy the natural light all day long. A pretty blonde, she welcomes you with a sweet smile that says, "You're beautiful just the way you came in, but have a seat and let's talk it over."

Suzanne loves hair color. And when she talks about it, while sitting in the dimming afternoon light in her living room, she splays out her fingers, separating out imaginary sections of hair to be brushed with color and then foiled. She is like a child weaving an imaginary cat's cradle. And it is easy to tell she likes the feel of her fingers as they bend, stretch, and twist to transform the hair only real in her mind's eye.

These are the same fingers that twenty-five years ago used to sep-

arate out her patient grandfather's hair and make little pigtails all over the elderly man's thinning scalp. This was the man who taught her her first and most enduring life lesson.

For a time while I was growing up, my grandfather was my surrogate dad. My father was an evangelist traveling around the country preaching at different churches, and he was only home twelve weeks every year. So my grandfather did everything with me.

My grandfather taught me to really enjoy and appreciate life. He taught me how to crochet, knit, and macramé. He taught me how to sew and to shoot guns. And he even took me up on my first airplane ride. He would sit on the couch and let me put hair clips, elastics, and braids in his hair, totally letting me do what I wanted.

For thirty years he worked as an electrician in a navy shipyard. He hated every minute of it.

He told me that no matter what I did in life to make sure I loved it. For some reason that piece of advice sank in. I never forgot it.

Her first job in a beauty salon near her New Hampshire home-town came not because she was a qualified stylist but because she had a dignified presence that would appeal to the salon's elite clientele where she served them . . . as a receptionist.

They had over 150 applicants, but they hired me. It was probably the way I looked: I had just come back from a trip to California; I was blond, young, tan, and thin. I was sharp-looking. They were very upscale and conservative. And they saw that I could sit behind the front desk and greet people with a smile and an intelligent voice.

The owner of the salon also had a very prestigious shop on Boston's Newbury Street. *Boston* magazine once did a feature on the fifty wealthiest people in Boston, and over thirty of those people were his clients. I almost died when I saw the Fiedlers in the reception book.

Being a receptionist at a salon is a difficult job, and I was clueless. We had eight different stylists, and they all worked differently. This person doesn't do perms, this person specializes in long hair styles; some booked every half hour, some needed longer appointments.

And, Suzanne quickly discovered, such an elite salon attracted temperamental stylists who flaunted their status and egos, often at Suzanne's expense.

The salon coordinator and five of the stylists were prima donnas. One of them even swore at me in front of the clients. And another would gossip about me, urging the clients to complain to the manager about me.

But I always got along with the manager and the owner, even though he was really a tyrant to work for. And one day he asked me if I wanted to train under him and be his assistant.

Becoming a hairstylist meant freedom to me. All day long I would sit behind my desk and watch these incredible hairstyles come out. I was always blown away by it: the colors, the cuts, the perms.

The owner was amazing. He was always on the cutting edge, always learning. And he was a real showman. He was high-end in his professionalism, the way he dealt with clients, what he expected of his stylists, and what he expected of his assistants. He was a perfectionist, and I always had respect for him and the work he put out. I knew it was a tremendous opportunity to be able to learn from him.

I worked for him for three years and received only two compliments. One night we were leaving at the end of a very long day. He handed me a wad of cash, which turned out to be $175. He simply said, "You did a really good job today and the clients love you."

One other time we were driving home from Boston and he said, "You know more about color than anyone else on the floor." I was only the assistant. I almost fell over.

But soon Suzanne had a difficult decision to make. To truly launch her career as a stylist, she had to leave the prestigious salon that gave her her start. And soon events helped her make her decision.

In New Hampshire you can get your license in two ways. You can go through a 2,000-hour and two-year apprenticeship, or you can go to school. And after a while, things weren't going well at the salon. If the owner ever got mad enough at me to fire me, what would I do? Not a lot of salons in the area needed an assistant.

The owner was teaching me all the wonderful things you usually learn after you get out of school, but I still needed the basics. I needed school to give me that. But I had to put myself through school, and the owner agreed to let me work at the salon part-time.

But I ended up quitting the salon after a falling-out over fifty dollars. The evening cash-out showed we were short by fifty dollars, and no one would fess up to it. So the owner said that since the cash drawer was my responsibility, he would take it out of my pay. But I had only been at the desk two hours that day.

But the incident also robbed Suzanne of her passion for this high-ego, high-drama profession, and she dropped out of school as well. The hiatus, however, gave her a chance to discover how passionately she wanted to resume her profession—and how everything else paled in comparison for her. What followed would be the most strenuous test of her energy, her artistry, and her determination.

I kept wondering if all salons would be that way. I was jaded, and the high pressure finally got to me. So I took a job at a department store cosmetics counter. And I hated it.

I couldn't be creative, and I felt people didn't treat me seriously. It simply wasn't my love, and I knew it.

At the same time I went back to the salon to get my nails done. And one of my friends told me, "You've got to finish and get your license. Go back now. If you don't, you'll never return to school."

So I went back to school, continuing to work part-time at the department store. For six months I worked fifty-five to seventy hours a week. I didn't have a car, so I took the bus from school to work to home.

My paycheck from the store paid my rent, and I lived off the tips I made from cutting hair at the school. I lived on french fries, peanut butter and crackers, and coffee that I got from friends who worked at the restaurant next door to my apartment.

For the most part I was totally focused. I had to go to work every day. I had to pay my bills. I had to feed myself. I had to take the bus. I had to graduate. Those were the things I knew I had to do. And I just did them without even thinking.

I was going after my dreams and not allowing myself to be held back.

But being treated so shabbily at the department store gave me the determination I needed to stick it out. I was getting very tired of being treated the way I was being treated. It finally dawned on me that I deserve to be treated better than this. That I'm not a bad person.

During her months of financial hardship and overwork, Suzanne's determination was tested by an invitation once again to leave school. But instead of being a temptation, that invitation gave her the chance to strongly define who she was and where she wanted to go with her calling.

The store where I worked also had an in-house salon. But the salesgirls who worked at the store came all the way to my school to have me do their hair—instead of going to their own salon!

The salon at the store offered me a job there, but I didn't want to do that. It was not the quality I was looking for. You can go either high-end or mediocre. Don't sell yourself short. Go with what your heart tells you to do, even if it means you have to wait a while longer.

The salon at the store was second rate, and I had known the first-rate salons. So I told them no. But they told me, "You won't make any money out there."

I've been in this business. I've worked on Newbury Street. I know where the money's at. The people who say it's not lucrative are the people who don't give it time, who don't have a love for it, or who aren't good at it. You just have to be patient.

Suzanne was patient. After graduation she moved south and be-gan to work at Ludwig's soon after passing her state boards. At this time, in her late twenties, her life truly began, with perhaps only a hint of conflict that is a relic from her past as the daughter of an evangelical father.

I get such a rush when I do someone's hair, when the person looks in the mirror and says, "Oh, that's exactly what I wanted." I get this feeling right in my chest, and I bebop around the whole day.

It's incredible. It's instant gratification. Especially with color. That's when you get to be an artist. I just love the feeling of getting my hands in the hair, of sectioning it out and bringing it up.

But I still have a really hard time with those old lessons I learned as a child—that vanity is a sin, that what's on the inside should be more beautiful than what's on the outside. I have a really hard time with that.

As far as I'm concerned, what I'm doing is basic upkeep. And I'm helping my clients feel good about themselves. They can look in the mirror and smile at what they're looking at.

That makes it easier to see what's on the inside and to like that as well.

I have a great job. I get paid to help people and make them feel good about themselves.

Part Three

BLESSINGS IN DISGUISE

Are you cursed with bad luck and disadvantages?
Or are you blessed with opportunities, insights, and
understandings that only your set of experiences
could allow you to have?
One way of looking at your life will drain your energy.
The other way will give you a power and a sense
of good fortune that moves you forward with faith
and gratitude. You have one life, but you have
at least two ways of looking at it.

12

Turn Handicaps
into Assets

The answer is <u>not</u> in the back of the book.

CHARLES "CHIC" THOMPSON

49, Creativity Consultant

A handicap is anything that keeps us from living our life to the fullest. A physical or mental disability. A judgment leveled against us based on the ignorance and prejudice of others. Our own harsh voice ticking off a list of shortcomings to hold us back. Any one of these can become the excuse for giving in to spirit-breaking depression and giving up on our dreams.

But if we let it, a handicap can serve as a catalyst for self-discovery and inner growth. It can provide the strength to start focusing on what we were born to do instead of indulging in magical thinking about what our life would be like if only . . .

There's no easy way to turn the handicaps in your life into assets. Instead, it will take all your focused determination and endurance to find and travel the path that is uniquely yours.

For Chic Thompson, the expressions "Yes, but," "It will never work," and "Don't rock the boat" are killer phrases that will snuff the life out of every idea—perhaps the very thought that could have saved a life, found a cure, or changed the world. Anyone attending Chic's seminars on creativity who dares to utter those dread expressions in the presence of this youthful man is likely to become the target of a red or green foam ball aimed directly at his head.

By the end of any day spent in his seminars, the room is thick with airborne balls. The rowdy participants could be schoolchildren or the highest-level executives from Andersen Consulting, Corning, Du Pont, GE, Hewlett-Packard, IBM, Price Waterhouse, the CIA, and the FBI. Here is where techniques for creative brainstorming are reborn in the oh-so-grown-up minds of America's thought leaders.

His philosophy: Creativity opens doors you never knew existed.

His mission: To give people the tools to become creative problem-solvers, to help them find all the right questions, develop new ideas successfully, and blast apart walls that confine our imagination and potential.

From South Bend to South Africa, Chic has been called upon to spark the creative fires in individuals all over the world. His rich baritone and earnest manner can turn a roomful of button-down executives into a group of excited children, chattering away with fresh ideas. It's as if Chic has simply reached inside their heads and flipped that switch from "I can't" to "I can." It happens that quickly.

I like to follow what Plato said: that you can achieve immortality by having children or creating new ideas. I've chosen the latter path.

I love ideas—you can explore them, massage them, put them on the shelf for a while, come back to them. And I'm convinced that the reason I'm successful is because none of my ideas have monetary faces on them. I never created an idea to make money. True, I've become a millionaire through my ideas and through my work helping others generate ideas. But the greater wealth has always been from the excitement I get from the creative process itself.

Most ideas come out of dumb questions. Creative problem-solving needs two ingredients: the adult's ability to define the problem, and a child's innocent willingness to look at the problem backward and forward and upside down.

Then you can use the adult approach to evaluate which ideas offer value.

While children are eager to tap into their imagination, adults will throw out killer phrases like "We're not coming up with anything" or "That's something a kid would dream up."

To me, the best question you can ask is "What would I never do?" when trying to solve a problem. Then you look at your list of your never-do's, turn them around 60, 90, or 180 degrees, and from that list come up with solutions that will help you succeed where no one else would.

Creativity is stifled at an early age, even though adults, their children, and their businesses best thrive when creativity is part of everyday life. Did you know that we're most creative at age five and least creative at age forty-four? That children hear almost 400 no's per day as opposed to fewer than 30 yeses? That the average child asks 65 questions a day, the average forty-four-year-old, only 5? And a five-year-old laughs 113 times a day, but the 44-year-old laughs only 11 times, for a lifetime average of 14.2 times a day.

That blows me away, and that's why I frequently start my presentations by saying, "We start school as question marks and graduate as periods. And that, as in life, is why the answer is *not* in the back of the book." Which is actually good news, because we each must use our creativity to build a one-of-a-kind life.

Think about it. Are our goals in education *really* the correct goals? Is a 4.0 in kindergarten going to make you successful, or is learning to be invaluable to yourself what you should strive for? I think Mark Twain said it best over a century ago: "Don't let formal education get in the way of learning."

Chic understands that message all too well. Formal education was a wrenching experience for him, for a reason he didn't fully comprehend until adulthood.

I was dyslexic, and I wasn't diagnosed until I was thirty. As a child, I knew I was smart, but nothing showed anyone that this was true. I knew I was good in sports, even though I was usually the shortest kid in class. Of course, I was never picked for teams because I was too small. I just always felt different.

And as I made my way through the educational system, it became worse. When you sit in class and can't comprehend, you begin to get really tired. Teachers told me if I didn't improve my reading I'd fail. So I tried extra hard, and my mother helped me with all my schoolwork and never made me feel stupid. But when I hit high school—*bam!*—

there were too many subjects, and I couldn't just get by on my personality anymore. Then, of course, the same thing happened in college.

Chic was soon to learn the meaning of paradox and the effect it would have again and again on his life.

But at the same time I kept being asked to accept leadership roles. It was like I always dreamed of power and then it was given to me, again and again. As a young boy, the priest at my church asked me to be an acolyte and read Scriptures every Sunday. But because I was dyslexic, I had to spend six nights a week memorizing the Scriptures.

In retrospect, that was probably the best strategy to get me into public speaking, putting a child in front of four hundred people in church! My freshman year at the University of Delaware I had to take ROTC. That was 1966, during the Vietnam War, and like most young people, I was struggling with my feelings about the war. I was a member of the ROTC *and* Students for a Democratic Society. And both groups kept appointing me to leadership positions!

Meanwhile, I was failing so many classes my freshman year of college that I was forced to enroll in the easy courses that many of the athletes took. One of the courses was public speaking—suddenly I had found a small niche. Every talk I gave I got an A. And I won the public speaking competition.

My first talk in that class was on smoking banana peels. I rolled a bunch, lit up, and talked about it. My second speech was on why men should be allowed to wear miniskirts. I stood on a table in class, calmly took off my trench coat, and there I was giving my talk wearing a miniskirt.

Everyone loved it, including me. I was commanding attention, getting A's, and having a blast. It felt totally natural. Then I would go from that class into History of Delaware, and I'd fail because I would try to read the textbook and I just couldn't get it. School was like a roller-coaster ride: the high of acing classes like public speaking and chemistry where I could use my ability to memorize the smallest detail, then the low of failing English and history.

Chic learned early that the conventional process of education wasn't going to teach him the things he would need to thrive in life. Those lessons and opportunities came from the people he met outside the classroom. A chance meeting on a tennis court was one of the first encounters to change his direction in life.

When you're dyslexic, you have to find something you

can excel in. For me it was sports and athletics, and those activities always felt right. Although I didn't travel in the kind of social circles that opened up high-level job opportunities, I've met a lot of people through being a tournament tennis player and, later, a golfer.

By my fifth year of undergraduate work I was still struggling toward my degree and having trouble with my foreign language requirements. Some might say if I'd spent less time on the tennis court and more time conjugating verbs I might have been out of school faster. But in my entire career I have been introduced to many opportunities through sports. And no one has ever asked me if I would conjugate any verbs for them.

I was playing tennis with a senior officer of W. L. Gore & Associates, the company that makes Gore-Tex, and he invited me to come over to the office to meet everyone and just do a courtesy interview. Within half an hour the president, Bill Gore, offered me a job as a research chemist, responsible for developing new products!

In the research lab at Gore & Associates, we had to sell our ideas to management and potential clients. My coworkers always volunteered me because I was good at giving presentations; it felt comfortable. I wasn't thinking yet that I would go into public speaking, but it just kept pulling me. I guess I was too busy dealing with the surprised look on clients' faces when I would show up in person to demonstrate a product. I was an adult voice on the phone, but I looked like a twelve-year-old.

"Short and young-looking" was yet another stigma Chic felt he had to deal with on a daily basis. He finally realized that only he could decide how he would let it affect him from now on.

Some people actually laughed in my face when they met me. To this day, that reaction still happens. When I gave a talk at Kraft General Foods, one of the executives told me that he had a sweater that was older than me. Now I choose to take that kind of remark as a compliment. I grew up trying everything I could to make people *not* think of me as short and young-looking. Public speaking was a perfect solution: what can make you feel taller than doing most of your work onstage? I'm three feet higher than everyone else!

Soon I decided I wanted to work for the Walt Disney Company because I had an idea to start a health education division that would use Disney cartoons. Naturally, everyone said, "You can't work for Disney." But I went in for an interview anyway, and when I pitched my idea, the company told me I was hired if I would go out and sell for a year. So I did, and I met all their sales goals. I also introduced the idea that Disney cartoons should be put on videotape. The president informed me that no cartoons would ever be placed on videotape as long as *he* was president. I quit the next week.

That experience showed me that I needed to have my own company to make my ideas happen. So I started an educational video production company with what I had—$500. I sold my car and moved into the bedroom of a house that I rented for $75 a month.

I was trying to decide what should be my first educational video, and at the same time my girlfriend was diagnosed with genital herpes. Nobody really knew what it was back then. That became my first video: *Herpe, The New VD Around Town.* No one wanted to buy it at first—I had trouble giving it away—but a few years later everyone in the country knew about herpes and the video finally started getting attention.

This is when I began to learn that to be successful, a creative idea should be only one step ahead of its time. In the early eighties I was brainstorming the idea for my next educational video with my neighbor, author Rita Mae Brown, when she leaned over and whispered, "AIDS." I called the Centers for Disease Control and learned that AIDS was going to be a pandemic.

I made a video on AIDS, but when I tried to market it,

the initial response was the same as it was with the herpes video—no one will want to see it; no one will want to buy it. The same thing happened with my videos on steroid use and cocaine abuse, but I had decided by then to follow my own instincts and keep producing these videos.

What really began to gel was this feeling of complete satisfaction from having an idea and seeing it accomplished. I met Dr. Elisabeth Kübler-Ross when she was using my AIDS video in her lectures on death and dying. It was clear that her purpose on earth was to reach out to help people, while for me the achievement of an idea was the natural fit.

The success of Chic's video production business meant that he would be wearing more than one hat—an expansion of his role that he felt fully capable of handling. Until financial disaster finally drove home the truth.

I had pretty good royalties coming in on my videos, and there were ten employees in my company. But then one day the company's banker called and told me that the IRS had frozen my bank account because the bookkeeper hadn't kept up withholding payments. I then discovered that my bookkeeper had embezzled $20,000. Plus I had hired someone as my vice president at twice my own salary and he had alienated everyone—I'd picked the wrong person.

My company had reached a point where I knew I couldn't go further with the managerial skills I had. I knew that to grow the company I had to live and breathe being a manager, but I also knew I didn't want to do that. That wasn't my calling. Focusing on ideas and how they click into the future was my calling.

So Chic set up a program that allowed his employees to buy him out. And he paid off his financial obligation within a year and a half. And he moved on. And forward.

I think we all learn by *not* doing it right the first time. Life's lessons are not failures. There's a temptation to be angry, to say, "Why me?" But it's also a motivation to get past the self-pity and move on.

Well, the way to move on was to ask myself, "Now what do I want to do?" And my immediate answer was that I wanted to give talks on creative motivation. I had to ask someone who did this for a living what he charged. He said $250, so I started charging that for my talks. Finally I began to do what now matters to me most—helping others unlock that internal creative process to make ideas happen!

Most people aren't self-sufficient, and that bothers the hell out of me. What *scares* me the most is the deep division I see between social classes. On my business trips, I fly first-class, I'm paid thousands of dollars for a seminar, I stay in five-star hotels, then I'm picked up in a limo and driven past neighborhoods where people's lives are filled with despair. I never have enough time, and I'm driven past people who have too much time. My life is changing every day; their lives never change. I see young people standing on the street corner selling drugs. Here they have these incredibly creative ways of selling their product, which are totally misplaced. That kind of paradox in life really angers me. How can we take that creativity on the street corner and use it in some positive way?

One answer came about when I was in Los Angeles during the riots after the Rodney King verdict. I was on a local radio talk show answering the question "How would you apply creativity to the LAPD's actions?" I invited listeners to discuss everything the LAPD did, then challenge those actions by doing the exact opposite and evaluating if there was any value to those opposite actions.

It was great—the callers really got into it, and we brainstormed about where kids go when everything's closed up. They head out to the street. What could you open up that would be a safe learning environment? Someone called in and said, "Well, you would *never* open a gun store." And I said, "Wait a minute, don't think linear. How could we make a gun store a learning experience for children?" Out of that discussion the idea for the "Guns for Toys" campaign in L.A. was born!

Chic credits his dyslexia and weak management skills for leading him to his calling. While others might view them as setbacks, Chic celebrates them as the catalysts to the success he enjoys now and the enlightenment he brings to others.

Sometimes people ask me if I get tired of giving motivational seminars, of saying the same things over and over. Never! Does a minister get tired of saying the Lord's Prayer? My talks are my personal bible. I'm always shaping and improving what I say, and each talk has different meanings for different groups.

Great ideas are always there inside each of us; they just need a catalyst to bring them out in the open. That's my role—showing people how to become their own catalyst for creativity.

13

Reject Fear

Only one thing in life is going to kill you.
Until then nothing else will.

VICTORIA McKERNAN

38, Mystery Writer

Fear is what keeps us safe. Too safe. While it might save our life, fear can also rob us of the colors, textures, and thrills that make life worth living. It can also seduce us into staying in what appears to be a secure situation. Don't be fooled by the illusion of security.

Before severe storms, ships leave their snug harbors and head out to open seas. Sometimes safety is found a long way from home.

Courage is a habit you build over time by exposing yourself to risk for the sheer fun and flavor of living. Then your fully developed sense of adventure will lead you safely down merry paths of unexpected good luck and right-place-at-the-right-time encounters.

And one day that well-practiced fearlessness will give you the strength to stand up straight and strong when your integrity, your self-respect, or even your calling is at stake. In the meantime you can have a lot of fun.

Chicago Nordejoong has a boa constrictor. So does Victoria Mc-Kernan. Chicago patches together a living. Victoria does, too—writing, taking on editorial odd jobs, serving food, or tending bar. Chicago's mother died when she was young, and she traveled around the world with her father on merchant marine vessels. Victoria lived with her parents and two sisters in a one-bedroom apartment in northern Virginia until she graduated from high school.

Chicago lives aboard the Tassia Far, *a wooden ketch built thirty years ago by her father. This ketch is permanently berthed inside Victoria's imagination, from which she spins the adventures of Chicago and her on-again, off-again lover, Alex, a retired government agent with a shady past. Chicago appears in three published novels, and now Victoria is writing her fourth mystery while she*

*lives alone with her snake, Thornton, in a two-bedroom condo-
minium in Washington, D.C. She lives in a rough part of town, but
it's within walking distance of some great bars, where she still pours
drinks now and then to take a break from her solitary writing life
and to bring in a little extra cash.*

*Like Chicago, Victoria has traveled around the world. And her
apartment, furnished mostly in secondhand furniture, futons, and
big cushions, is decorated with the loot of her travels and many interests. By her sofa a stand holds skulls of a beaver, a goat, a bison,
a cougar, and a caribou that she found in Ireland, North Dakota,
Alaska, Belize, and Montana.*

*Her own patrician cheekbones frame large aqua eyes. As she sits
on the floor and stretches her long legs, her pants cuff slides up her
ankle to reveal a fantastically colored tattoo of a bird. It's the "glori-
ous scar of flight," she says, referring back to the dream that inspired
it. It's a metaphor for her life.*

I dreamed I was in Singapore or Malaysia watching people flying fabulous kites, and I saw this kite lying on the
ground made of heavy logs. It was obvious no one was going to be able to fly it, but I thought I'd give it a try. It took
off in the wind, and the string was reeling out so quickly I
lost control of it and tried to step on it. It slit my ankle
down to the bone. Everyone gathered around and said
how horrible it looked and that I should rush to the doctor
to have it closed. But the doctor said it was always going to

be open like that. The scar looked like a long, beautiful feather, so I drew it when I woke up.

About the same time I had that dream, my father gave me money to buy a coffeemaker for my thirtieth birthday. I instead took the money to a tattoo artist who said she could put my feather on my ankle. (When I saw what beautiful work she could do, I asked for a whole bird.) That feather seems to represent my life, wide open and seeming to need to be closed up with security and a real job. But I also know it's destined to stay open, no matter how many people tell me I should get it fixed. And the kite? It looked impossible to fly, but I felt, in my dream, why not give it a try? What did I have to lose? And how would I know until I tried?

I've worked thirty different jobs all around the world, working in a factory, picking cucumbers, even dancing in an opera. My security is knowing I can go anywhere in the world, get a job, and generate income as I need it. Most people don't have any idea how easy it really is to find some kind of work.

I feel silly and fraudulent saying that I have some great truth, but the best lesson I can pass on is that nothing much is going to kill you. If you start there you can put up with anything, and you will be able to develop an adaptability to any situation you find yourself in. And there will always be something interesting in life to explore.

Victoria's adventure streak began as it begins with most American children, in her home while she watched television. But unlike most American teenagers, who spend their money on music and clothes, her dream of free wanderings drove a single-minded frugalness that bought her way to the road as an eighteenth-birthday present.

The difference in our lifestyle, being five people crowded in a small one-bedroom apartment, with no real place to play or other children to play with, was one of the major factors in my longing to escape and explore.

By the time I had graduated from high school, I had literally never been anywhere. My mother was probably mentally ill, and my father was working full-time and served as both mother and father to three children. But he took us to Ocean City for a day in the summer, and spent the weekends and evenings sharing with us everything Washington had to offer. When most fathers want to relax in front of the TV at night or play golf on weekends, he took us to the museums, the library, the zoo, hundreds of free concerts and Shakespeare plays. We were exposed to a lot more of the world through books and concerts and stories than most children.

He was also tremendously influential on the development of my desire to explore, as he had hitchhiked around

as a young man and worked at a bunch of odd and interesting jobs before settling down. He told us stories of his
war years in North Africa, which basically consisted of
hanging around gambling with the natives and eating an
aspic of wild boar that had been shot by Winston
Churchill. He was, in fact, one of the few soldiers ever to
go AWOL at the end of his tour, taking off for a card game
in Casablanca the day before they were supposed to go
home.

One of my earliest stirrings toward adventure came
from playing with his wristwatch, because he had won it in
a card game in Iceland, where he had gone to build an airport. The stories of his travels and the whole image of Iceland were so foreign and exotic that this was a huge factor
in my life.

My early influences were the images on *The Wonderful
World of Disney* of families traveling to Yosemite in their station wagons. I also remember looking at pictures of tents
in the Sears catalogs, thinking, Wow, with a tent you can
just go anywhere. There was a lot I wanted to see and find
out about. So I worked in my spare time, never bought
clothes or records, and by the time I graduated from high
school I had saved enough money to buy an old school bus
from the Safari Day Camp. It still had "Safari" painted on
the side, and I knew it was an omen immediately. So I

painted the van with zebra stripes and drove it around the country for three years.

But that very first night she learned her first and probably most important lesson, one that would see her safely around the world.

Like a typical teenager, I went to the beach right away and thought I would spend the night on the sand. As I walked along, carrying my blanket and pillow, I felt something brush my leg. I walked a few more steps, and it brushed again! For some reason I was convinced it was an orangutan, so I dropped my blanket and ran away. Then I realized it was just my blanket brushing my leg! So I got my first lesson that very first night: Sometimes your fear is just your blanket.

The issue of safety has been an interesting one for me. In all my travels I have never been threatened. I would even pick up hitchhikers on the road. I give off an openness and matter-of-factness with people. I figure maniacs are going to get you anywhere—you don't have to be actually traveling to encounter them—and everyone else you can deal with. Sure I've met weird people and a few oddballs now and then, but then you just learn to handle it.

The people and adventures Victoria encountered would eventually fuel her writer's imagination. Her job, she says, was to learn as much as she could about the world.

When I left, I had $1,500 saved up. I headed for Canada,

then looped through the Midwest and wound up in Arkansas, where I got involved with some charismatic Christians and stayed with them for a while. I saved up more money working at a racetrack there for a season. After buying a second van, I continued traveling west, where it broke down in California, close to the Mexican border. I ended up staying in California with a guy I picked up hitchhiking. We spent two weeks rebuilding my engine, and I helped deliver his girlfriend's baby in a cabin in the woods.

Some people would have called me a homeless person, a vagabond, in those days. But I felt that I was doing my job: traveling and learning as much as I could before going to college. I had always intended to go to college, so I never saw this time as just bumming around. I kept a journal all the time and wrote sketches, stories, and impressions of what I encountered on my travels. I wasn't expecting to get any of them published, but I was beginning to think that I might want to become a novelist. But I still didn't know what I wanted to write about.

After three years of driving around North America, family issues, illnesses, and her own craving for the intellectual challenge of more formal education called her home. And she took on the adventure of buckling down to formal studies and being a conventional student. But soon the road called again. And step by step, the road revealed itself before her. Not always knowing what the next step would be or where the next ticket would take her, she found that each new experience reaffirmed her confidence that she'd survive the next.

By the time I came home to go to school at George Washington University, I was settled down but still not very focused. I thought that I might even study to become a physician. GW offered journalism and theater as well as a respectable med school. And since I found that I had begun craving intellectual challenge and structure, I settled into studying.

I finished college in three years, working nights as an EKG technician, then kept that job for the next year as I began to seriously work on my writing. This was a great job because I could study during my shift, and I began to seriously work at my typewriter during the day. No, I didn't know anything about being an EKG technician before I started the jobs, but with all the jobs I'd had while traveling, I'd come to decide that most jobs weren't that hard. So when someone asks me if I can do something, I say yes and then go try to figure it out.

But as I wrote during the day, I started getting that feeling that I still didn't have enough to say. It was frustrating trying to write stories based on some kind of truth that I knew I didn't yet know. So again, I just packed everything up, sold what I could, and began traveling around the world. Since my tuition had been covered by my father's savings and some free credits that I had earned by working at the university hospital, I had graduated debt-free and was able to save the money I needed to travel more.

By the time I reached Greece that first winter, I had only $100 left, a EurailPass that was good for only three more days, and there was a possible ferry strike that could leave me stranded in Greece. It was getting cold, and I didn't want to spend the winter hitchhiking through Italy and Greece. My other option was to pick oranges with other migrant workers for the season, but that's a sleazy scene. So I was beginning to feel stuck.

There I was sitting in the ferry terminal wondering how I was going to get out of the country, when I picked up a copy of the *International Herald Tribune*. There was an ad for an au pair to work for the winter in St. Moritz. I thought to myself, That's my job. I'm going to go get it.

The ferry finally sailed on the last day of my pass. When I got to Zurich, I phoned the lady from the train station. But she said she'd already found an Austrian woman and was hoping for a man to help shovel snow and do the heavy work. I told her, "I'm as strong as a man," and she laughed and agreed to meet me. I washed my hair in the train station bathroom, put on the skirt I had just bought in Greece for the interview, and got the job.

They weren't going to need me for another week, so she

said, "Where do you want to go? I'll buy you a ticket to get there and back." So I naturally picked Paris. Of course, I had no money in Paris, but it was okay because I had the *idea* of money in my immediate future. So I ate bread and cheese and stayed in a youth hostel with Algerian students.

In St. Moritz the chalet had fourteen bedrooms, and a lot of people would stay. During my winter there I met great international artists, jet setters, and Greek tycoons. Although I was the servant, there would be whole periods where there wasn't much to do, so I would go out back and put on some skis.

I didn't know how to ski when I arrived in St. Moritz, and there wasn't anyone to teach me. But the hill I could see from the house looked manageable. I didn't have any idea that the lift continued on up to an expert run! I spent about half that first run on my butt, but I did get down the hill. You can always figure out a way of getting through a predicament, even if it means bumping downhill on your ass.

I would come home many times very sore, cold, and wet. It wasn't pleasant, but it wasn't fatal. I'm pretty good at risk assessment and just figured that I wouldn't die skiing. It's a lot harder to kill ourselves than we think. Only one thing in life is going to kill you, and until then nothing else will.

I earned so much money that winter that I began thinking, There's the whole rest of the world. There's no reason for me to go back right away. I had enough money to buy a ticket that would begin in London, with stops in Delhi, Singapore, Sydney, New Zealand, Tahiti, and finally end in Los Angeles. So I hitchhiked to London for the ticket.

After flying to Delhi, I went overland to Nepal, where I spent a month trekking. I knew I'd only have enough money to live for a couple of months in Asia, which was pretty cheap. And I knew that by the time I got to Australia I would have to find work. But I figured that would be easy enough. In the meantime I spent another month in Southeast Asia, where I hitchhiked in Malaysia, which is a good place for hitchhiking. They're respectful of women, and there are a lot of Chinese men in Mercedeses who like to practice their English.

Understanding came in more forms than simply crossing language barriers. Empathy, sympathy, and tolerance—three important instruments in the writer's toolbox—came as she worked side by side with people she never would have met in the suburban home of her teenage years.

I had run out of money again by the time I landed in Sydney. I was expecting a money order for $200 from the sale of some remaining possessions back home, but it hadn't arrived yet. I met up with some South American bongo players, partied all night with them, and stayed at a youth hostel that first night. At five in the morning I heard, "Does anybody want to work today? I have a landscaping job."

By dawn I had a shovel in my hand and was landscaping at a radar station. By the end of the day I had $50 in my pocket. This was sheer physical labor, and I would come home at night crushed, my whole body aching from twelve hours with a pick and shovel.

Up until then I had been a little scornful of the so-called unwashed masses. Why don't they better themselves instead of just lying around watching TV and drinking beer every night? Why not take classes, go to lectures, read books? But after twelve hours with a pick and shovel, all I wanted was beer, rest, a can of spaghetti, and a little mindless diversion too.

I worked a variety of jobs in Sydney for a couple of months, saved money, then got on as crew with a yacht sailing north. I had never sailed, but again, it was a case of "say you can and then figure out how." I was seasick for the next six weeks, but got to learn a new skill and explore lots of remote islands.

I left the yacht in Cairns, and after about a month of waitressing work, I was in the kitchen of my group house making macaroons when a stranger showed up with a job offer as a cook, first mate, and guide on his charter yacht. How could I turn down an opportunity like that! For the next couple of months I lived aboard that boat with the Coral Sea as my backyard.

Those months on the boat were perfect. I felt a real sense of peace, a certain fulfillment. I had come a long way and learned a lot. And soon I realized I was ready to go home. I was tired of being footloose and felt ready to move on with the next phase of my life, to really work at being a writer.

Although Victoria had put her footloose days temporarily behind her, she put flexibility and writing first, before so-called job security and an office job.

When I got back to Washington I immediately looked for a restaurant job. A job in a restaurant or bar is one of the best ways to earn a living while working on your art. You choose the hours you want to work, you work really hard for a short period of time, make a lot of money, and then have time out. It's active and fun, especially when you do something as solitary as writing for a living. It's nice to go out and see people and get paid for it at the same time.

I decided to write a mystery novel because I knew it would be easier to sell and because I thought it would be a good exercise. I also happened to have a good plot idea involving smuggling cocaine in scuba tanks. I was bartending, and one of my regular customers had an old roommate who was living with a *Miami Vice* producer. When I told her my plot idea, she suggested I work up a treatment for an episode, and promised that she would pass it along. While I never heard anything from the producer, I had a complete story outline. So I developed it into my first book, *Osprey Reef.*

After three mysteries now, I sometimes wonder when I will get back to serious work on my non-genre novel. But while my ultimate goal, of course, is to write really great enduring prose, I have come to appreciate the mystery genre and lose my literary elitism. You can't read *War and Peace* every day. Sometimes it's just nice to have lighter reading.

Literature is an extremely strong, potent, wonderful force. Many people list *To Kill a Mockingbird* as a life-changing book. The characters and story are so strong, but really, it is just a story. It was made up.

That is a powerful thing. Someday I might write the important novel that will touch people's hearts. I'm certainly going to try. But if my publishing success remains just with the mysteries, that will be okay, too. It isn't bad to just entertain people and maybe challenge them in little ways.

This is a whole other journey I'm on now: the writer's life, full of its own doubts and fears, adventures and loneliness. But it's the one I've chosen. And all those years of travel? They were a prologue to now. I have always had a vision that there was a purpose for my life. I didn't now what it was, but I knew it was something. Now I know.

14

Learn from Shame

*We spend too much time worrying about what
we _think_ we should be doing or where we should be
in our lives and in our careers.*

CHUCK BEVINS

50, Used-Car Salesman

We've all felt the familiar hot flush on our cheeks when
we've said or done something that we know is unworthy of
us. Or when we've knowingly participated in something
we sense deep down is wrong.

Shame. You know how it feels and how embarrassing it
can be to witness someone else's shame. Even children experience that sharp stab of regret before they can put a
name to it.

But shame can be a powerful teacher on the path to your calling. It reminds you that your uniqueness does not make you special or infallible. Instead, it's a wake-up call for change.

Sometimes it's our worst mistakes that lead us to higher ground.

The son of a West Virginia coal miner, Chuck Bevins is an admitted graduate of the school of hard knocks—married four times, with a less than stellar credit history, and making a living as a used-car salesman.

Chuck was introduced to shame early on in his life, in the form of what he calls "harsh physical discipline from my father." Barely in his teens, he ran away, using money he had saved for a one-way bus ticket to Chicago. Alone and afraid, he spent several months crying himself to sleep every night in a tiny kitchenette. He had to lie about his age to get work.

Decades later, Chuck has the face of a man who has worked hard for a living. He was a traffic cop, grocery store employee, and pastor before finally settling in to car sales, an occupation that carries its own shameful reputation. Chuck is familiar with the used-car salesman stereotype—loudmouthed liar in a plaid jacket.

Frankly, Chuck just isn't embarrassed anymore over who he is or what he does for a living. Hard times have taught him a valuable lesson: that peace of mind comes only when he's helping others, not when he's wrapped up in his own worries. That's why selling cars is a vocation that suits him—every day is a new opportunity to help people find the car that's right for them and a chance for Chuck to change their minds about what it means to be a car salesman.

The life I've led has given me an important asset—empathy for other people. I've been there. I know what bad credit is. I know what divorce is. I know what it's like to get down through no fault of your own. I understand when people come in to buy a car and have lousy credit, or have just been left by a husband or wife and have fallen on hard times.

That's why it's so important to me to know my customers—to see them as more than just a wallet I can sell a car to. I want to find out exactly what they need and what they can truly afford. I usually have to dig a little, because people won't tell the truth when they're embarrassed about bad credit; they'll try to hide it. If they start to hedge, I just say, "Don't feel bad; I've been there too." It always helps to know someone else understands your situation and the pain it causes.

Chuck is well aware of the fact that he's in a field of work whose reputation suffers, a reputation he says both the business and the customers are partly to blame for.

I've been selling cars for ten years now. I don't know how else to say this except to put it plainly: the car business can be a whore business. Management has a history of being cutthroat in how they deal with their employees, and there's no loyalty between the two. Many of the dealership owners expect their sales force to work all the time, but they don't pay fairly or show appreciation for the extras we do on the job.

I remember working for an owner and coming in on my own on Sundays to open up and make sure the place was clean. I didn't have to do that. Not only were there no thank-yous from the boss, he acted like that was the way it was supposed to be. Then one day he fired me, out of the blue. Maybe he heard I had been asked to work for another dealership, but I would never quit without giving notice, because I believe in being loyal to my employer. In any case, he didn't bother to find that out. He just fired me, for no good reason.

Now, on the other end you have the customer who will spend hours with you—right up to the point of purchase—then buy a car somewhere else because that dealership beat your price by $25! Everyone talks about salespeople and their lies, but I've found that the consumer is often the biggest liar who ever walked through the door! It's embarrassing sometimes.

Chuck believes that what's taking place in car sales is a reflection of the shameful state the world of work is in. He says America's employers must change the way they run their companies to undo the damage they've caused in the workforce. And he has plans to be part of that change.

I've always believed that if you're loyal and work hard, you can make it. That strong work ethic came from my parents. They taught me that nothing's free. When there was a downturn in the mines, my father cut grass and hedges. There were no free rides.

But over the decades I think we've all seen America's work habits go down to nothing, and loyalty right along with them. What can you expect? I've worked alongside individuals who came in late, didn't do the work, and still got paid the same salary I made. And sometimes they were even promoted!

I predict in the next fifteen to twenty years you're going to see companies becoming more loyal to their employees. Competition is so fierce that it's the employers who treat their workers fairly who will keep the best people. I hope to be part of that. That's why I'm working toward having my own dealership.

My dealership will be different because I'm going to take care of the people who work for me and treat them with respect. And I won't be open on Sundays. It's a day of worship for many people, and everyone needs time off to be with family and loved ones. I know other dealerships are open all the time, trying every sales gimmick to bring people in, but I believe that if you run an ethical business and treat people with respect, most of the time they'll do the same to you.

I feel needed at the dealership where I work now, by both the customers and the management. I'm treated with respect and paid fairly for my work. And the funny thing is, if it weren't for getting fired from my last job, I probably wouldn't be here! I really believe that things happen for a reason.

"Things happen for a reason" is a frequent phrase in Chuck's conversations. He says his life has been marked by events—some good, some bad—to constantly remind him that he's on this earth to be of help to others.

My father was a religious man, but his manner of discipline—he could get very violent. My mother was strong, but my folks had a traditional marriage, and she always recognized my dad as the head of the household. I remember him working the 2-to-11 shift in the mines and my mom baking pies at night. The first piece she cut, she always set aside for my father. He was from the old school that didn't respect women like he should have. I was just fifteen when I ran away, and I didn't tell anyone but my mom, because I didn't want her to worry.

Years later, when I came home for a visit, my father apologized for his behavior. I kept thinking, if he hadn't been the way he was, who knows? Maybe I would have stayed, gotten mixed up with the wrong crowd, and ended up in the penitentiary like one of my buddies from school. Things happen for a reason.

I remember working in the city traffic division of the police department when I broke my back on the job. I was in bed for months. One day I picked up the Bible on the nightstand and began reading. From that moment on, I learned what it really means to have faith, to ask God every morning, "You know where I need to be today, so please give me the strength to get there."

That wasn't the first time God was trying to get through to me. As a young boy I felt a calling to be a pastor. I was too young to understand why, but I had this feeling that that was what God wanted me to do. It kept me focused over the next several years, to try as hard as I could in school and stay out of trouble. I actually did become a pastor for a while in my thirties. It was a small church that had gone through four pastors in two years. Once again I felt that this was happening to me for a reason, that this was where God wanted me to be. While I was there, we built a new sanctuary and enrolled over a hundred children in Sunday school.

Pastoring helped me define my own purpose—to help people who are heavy with the cares of life get relief and hope. It was the greatest high for me.

But then I left it when I left my first wife. I felt like I didn't have the energy or the right to minister to anyone anymore. The divorce left me depressed and angry about my life.

But I can do either one of two things. I can look back and see what I've been through and use it to be a better person today, or I can see it as a stumbling block to hold me back.

Chuck's dedication to helping others earned him the lead in a major newspaper column when a family wrote in to praise him for the kindness and concern he showed for their little girl when she threw up in his office. Not only did he clean up the mess himself, but when the little girl began crying because she had also gotten sick all over her favorite doll, he offered to wash and dry the doll for her. To the family's surprise, he gave them a new car to test-drive, taking a big risk that the car would not return in the same state of cleanliness.

It turned out that the family didn't buy a car from Chuck, but that was all right with him.

That newspaper column was a surprise, especially since I

was just trying to help. When the columnist called me about the letter, I told him, "I was just trying to serve the people; you don't go through this life but one time."

But a lot of people will help others only if they can be recognized for it. There was a janitor named Bubba at one of the car dealerships where I worked. The other employees looked down on him because he was "just" a janitor, but I always treated him with respect. I remember it was a cold, wet day and I noticed he had holes in the bottoms of his shoes—you could see his socks. I mentioned it to him and he said, "Chuck, this is all I have."

I knew exactly what he was talking about because at the time I was going through a divorce and owed the IRS around $10,000. I told the general manager that I needed to take Bubba off the lot at lunchtime. I bought him a pair of insulated work boots, and that should have been the end of it. But one of the sales guys noticed his new boots and asked him where he got them. He said that I bought them for him. They got angry with me because I didn't tell them so that they could make a big show of taking up a collection to buy his boots!

Well, the next day the IRS sent me one of those threatening "you owe us money" letters, and I knew I was in trouble. At the time I was dating the woman I'm married to now, and on a lark I played her address in a local lottery. I won $36,000! I paid all my bills *and* bought a house for us. You see how things happen for a reason?

The road to becoming a Good Samaritan has been long and bumpy for Chuck, but it's a journey that has given him enlightenment and peace along the way.

I believe everybody has a blueprint in life, that God has an individual plan for each one of us. But within that blueprint is our free will to choose, and whatever we choose in life, we have to accept the responsibility that goes along with the choice. You look at your life and, yes, maybe some of your decisions have not been the best, but you go on with what you've got, for it ultimately puts you back on course.

The trouble is, most of our problems are self-inflicted, and yet we run around trying to blame other people every time something goes wrong.

No wonder most people don't have peace of mind. We've got to get away from being so competitive and possessive on an individual basis. When you're possessive, you lose what you're trying to hold on to. I've already been the route of having to drive a new car and needing everyone to like me. Well, you know what? A Volkswagen will get me from point A to point B; I don't need a Cadillac. And even though it would be nice if everyone I met liked me, if they don't, that doesn't mean I have to change how I feel. And I can still wish them the best. But so many people won't do that; their egos won't let them.

We spend too much time worrying about what we *think* we should be doing or where we should be in our lives and in our careers. I know now I could work in a 7-Eleven and be content. As long as I'm helping others, the job setting doesn't matter.

15

Bless Your Past

*You have to bless those people who were so unkind
to you that you just had to get out.*

LINDA FRAZIER

45, Television Executive

Over the last twenty years millions of Americans have discovered that they weren't alone in growing up in painful families. Many families have suffered alcoholism, drug addiction, domestic violence, or any number of dysfunctional and secret conditions that burdened young Americans for generations.

To know you're not alone is only the first step in reclaiming your life from the past. However, the way you come to terms with your past will determine the adult you become and how you express yourself in all areas of life—including work.

Tune in to Discovery Channel and chances are you will be transported into a world you will probably never visit in person. A grain of dirt from a spider's point of view. A computer motherboard. The human reproductive system. The Galápagos Islands. Many youngsters dreaming of a high-adventure career have found at Discovery Channel their chance to venture out to the most remote reaches of the planet and report back to the living rooms of America all that they see and learn.

As a Discovery Channel vice president, Linda Frazier inhabits the modern suburban building that houses the network offices. She carries her adventure within her in memories and recoveries. Discovery Channel represents the latest chapter in her story of self-sufficiency and hope. And, perhaps, the jumping-off place from which she can begin to take that hope to others.

Linda's working life has been a series of callings, each one taking her to an unknown destination, but teaching her valuable lessons that prepare her for her next assignment.

I'm in a company whose mission is to help people explore their world. Not everyone is going to be able to get to India; not everyone is going to be able to get to Egypt or experience cryonics up close or witness an operation. So we bring those experiences to our audience.

In the same way, I'm fulfilling a larger mission of my own. My journey from being a single mom with only a high school education to being a vice president at Discovery has given me the credibility to speak about my own story. This success is now making it possible for me to give back through speeches and through writing that we all have a calling and a path to follow.

It may look different at different times and in different ways. But we are really always on a path. I'm still on my path, and I still don't know where all of this is leading me to. I just have to accept that each step of the way, each day, I've got to give back a lot of what I've learned myself.

Learning is not a value that was instilled in Linda from a young age. The daughter of a father whose third-grade education limited his own dreams of life's potential and a mother who reached tenth grade, she grew up in a household that did the best it could with limited resources—both educationally and emotionally. For reading material, the family had a Bible and a few copies of the National Geographic. *Her father, who earned the family's income as a garbage collector, and uncles regularly used alcohol to escape their frustrations. Linda knew at a very young age that alcoholism, igno-*

rance, and abuse were playing a large role in the way she learned to build relationships—lessons not easily or quickly unlearned.

At seven I knew what I didn't want to be. We had generations of abuse running through both sides of the family. I didn't want to be bitter when I grew up. I didn't want to live my parents' life of struggle. But in order to belong, you are almost motivated to stay where you are so you don't lose what you do have. The risk is too great.

It was clearly not a childhood that I would design for my own children. But how can I judge my parents? My dad had an alcoholic and bitter father. He had a mother who was a martyr. My mom's mom died when she was eight. And she had a bitter and abusive father. What kind of role models did they have?

As much as she knew what she didn't want, at the age of eighteen Linda married it anyway: a young man she passionately loved but who continued those terrible family traditions. And her passage into her young adulthood began with terrible years. Years she is grateful for because they gave her her son and daughter.

I knew I didn't want some aspects of my father's behavior in a husband, but I was familiar with all the steps to the dance called alcoholism. When you know all the steps, you are comfortable with them. So when I met a really healthy man, I didn't know any of the steps, so I couldn't dance with him. When I met my first husband, whom I fell madly in love with, I saw that he didn't look like my father, didn't act like my father, and, boy, could we dance.

It took seven years to get so low as to finally realize I couldn't stay, that in order to be healthy I had to be willing not to be in a dance where I understood the steps. I had to leave my comfort zone.

One night there was an episode in my household I couldn't ignore. It was my last straw. I remember it was winter in New Jersey, and I ran out of the house without a coat on. It was a physically and emotionally traumatic event.

That night as I ran through the streets of my neighborhood crying, I had a talk with God. I said, "Okay, God, I took vows for better or worse. And I kept to that. But I don't think that this is what you meant. This 'worse' is too bad. So you either give me the strength to stay here and fix it, or you show me a way out. But I give up. It's in your hands."

Within a week the miracles happened. I tried the welfare system, and it didn't work. Then I went to my church, and all these doors opened. The church helped me get an apartment and gave me food baskets. They put my daughter in child care. I said, "Thank you, God. I asked and you answered, and I'm not going to let you down." And that was the beginning of my exit.

But unfortunately it also wasn't the end of the abuse. Even though I left the situation, the harassment and all the elements of the abuse continued. Every week he would come to my apartment, stand outside my window, and holler humiliating things for my neighbors to hear.

The first year any woman leaves a violent domestic relationship is particularly dangerous for her. In a moment of new strength, she's made the decision to leave. And now she has to try to hold on to that strength as she rebuilds her life, all the while wondering if maybe she did the wrong thing by leaving. At the same time the man is feeling threatened because he feels his control over her slipping away from him. This is the time when domestic violence–related murder happens most. Because if he can't have her, he must make sure no one else will either.

Which isn't to say that I was in that kind of danger from my first husband. But his continuing abuse left me no choice but to leave town. So I soon decided to take my children to Florida and start life over in a safer place.

Peripheral vision landed Linda her first job. Heading for a Tampa temporary-help service with two children in tow, and after having slept in her moving truck the night before in the city's red-light dis-

trict, she spotted a hotel next to the agency advertising the need for front desk help. Stressed, tired, and distracted by the young children sitting in the waiting room, she did not impress the temporary-help service. So she went next door. Because she had a smattering of hotel experience in New Jersey, she was hired for three dollars an hour to work the hotel desk. And this is where she began to discover herself through the lessons she learned dealing with hotel guests. No job, she discovered early, was too small or too menial to give her valuable gifts that would see her through her life and career.

During that time I could have made money in many ways that were just not congruent with my integrity. At that point my calling was to decide what kind of individual I wanted to be.

My source of joy during that time was the kids and knowing that every day they were okay and that the daily stress of the environment that we had in New Jersey was gone. We could wake up every day and feel safe. There was nothing that could be as bad as where I'd come from.

But I also discovered the psychology of finding myself through my work. Every job I've had since those days taught me something I needed to learn. At the hotel I learned how to begin to draw boundaries.

On the front desk it's your job to get yelled at. And there's a skill about not taking it personally. To be able to learn to empathize with their situation but not internalize it. Not take on the emotion of it, but find solutions to their problem. You have to decide at what point you're not going to accept that person's anger. How do you empathize and solve his problem and still be a whole person who is respected?

I ended up building such a loyal clientele that my career progressed in the hotel industry. When I changed hotels, companies like Kodak and Polaroid would take their business to my new hotel. I eventually was valued on how many room nights followed me. When I went to pitch for another job, I wasn't just a desk clerk. I was a desk clerk with a following.

People started telling me, "Linda, you've got to be in sales. We stay wherever you are."

A new career meant a new life in a new state. And all this required a leap of faith for Linda. A leap that would be rewarded.

I've never known what my career track was. All of us wonder at times, Where am I going? When I outgrew the hotel industry, I still didn't know what was next.

We all have open doors all the time. Whether we have the courage to walk through those doors because we don't know where they will take us, well, that's another thing. It's like walking through nothingness.

In the hotel industry I was on a salary. But then I went to a sales job—commission only. And I had kids to support! I had to know in my deepest heart of hearts that God always does provide. And I have never, never felt lack. That doesn't mean I always had what I wanted, but I never lacked the bare essentials. And I was under the poverty line for six years.

Society's scorecard is money, title, and professions. You can't ignore that when it's part of the world we live in. Does it mean something? Sure. Is it a goal? It is in the sense that the more money you make, the more things you can provide for your family. But I never really worried about money.

In her early days in sales, Linda was quickly snapped up by the cable industry, soon helping to develop a young MTV and eventually moving on to Discovery Channel. She has developed a close circle of friends, made up of some of the earliest women in cable television, and they continue to remain a close-knit group, each member receiving the necessary support and constructive input as she handles what life gives her.

I have grown up with these women, and if we could replicate what we are to one another, we could truly change the world. There is a total openness from a spiritual, professional, and personal level where the feedback is nonjudgmental. Our relationships are noncompetitive and based on unconditional love. And that means the world to me. I have truly grown through that.

I also have tried to create that at work. I took my entire department on a retreat this summer to experience teamwork. I told them, "I can't train you to be a team, but if you can feel what it's like to be on a team, you won't want it to be any other way." But it's hard to keep it alive, and you need a lot of reinforcement in the workplace.

But as she has developed this set of friends, remarried and begun a new family life, and pursued a dynamic career as an executive for an exciting cable network, she sees whatever the future holds for her as still rooted deeply in the past. What she brings from those years helps her immeasurably in being the woman she is today. Appreciation for the lessons is one gift.

What I learned at that hotel front desk I continue to use today, only on a different level. Everyone who works at this company is my customer. When they're angry because the systems and processes and the funding opportunities don't appear to be addressing their needs so they can fulfill their missions, I must use those same skills.

I have to manage and facilitate conversations to resolve conflicts at the very highest corporate level. When you're a facilitator, you have to be willing to be invisible and let the customer be right. I'm actually very excited about mastering this skill.

I absolutely feel like I'm doing God's work every day. Do I know what His plan is? I'm clueless. But I believe every human being on this planet is a thread in His tapestry. And we all have a role. If one of us doesn't do his part, it's like cutting a thread, and it will all eventually unravel.

And part of her thread, Linda believes, is showing through her own life that it's possible to thrive and prosper—even with a disadvantaged beginning.

I'm just a tool, I'm not really the whole story. I am an example. People tend to believe experiential stories more than academic stories. I'm credible because I lived it.

I do believe my work will affect the strengthening of the family unit through self-sufficiency. I don't think I have the power, credibility, or influence to change the world, but I might touch a couple of people. And I might not even make any effect on this generation. It may be the next generation that does change the world, and maybe that generation was touched by a mother that I touched.

So my goal is to touch as many as I can by the example that I set and in a way that is loving and honest and kind. I don't know how I'm going to be used for this purpose but it's there.

And part of her example is to show that forgiveness is indeed possible. No matter what.

When things were really bad, I always knew that I should figure out how they were a blessing. If my first marriage hadn't been so bad, I probably would have stayed.

And if I'd stayed, what would I have passed to my children? You have to bless those people who were so unkind to you that you just had to get out. It has to be bad enough that no matter what is out there, it is better than the present.

As far as my parents are concerned, I feel like I have honored them. As much as there has been bad stuff, there's been good stuff too. I was forced to look inward for my own inner drive because they could not support me.

They must have done something good, even if they only lopped off some of my hard edges, like a diamond in the rough.

I took what good they did and really embellished it. Now I give it to my kids, and hopefully they will do it for their children. That's the only way we can stop the generational passing of illiteracy, abuse, and alcoholism. We each have to cut off our rough edges for the next generation.

16

Resist Temptation

*I don't need no ultimatums. Money is great,
but only if you enjoy making it.*

DEXTER ACCARDO

45, Police Officer

As you pursue your calling, you will show a single-minded determination that might worry the friends and family who are close enough to notice your transformation. And they may try to help you return to "normal" by offering enticements to change your mind. Their friendship. Your marriage. Money. Anything that is important to them, they will put it on the line. It will be your choice: them or your calling. Choose wisely.

New Orleans and the parishes surrounding the city are a study in contrasts. Strong religious convictions. Stripper joints on Bourbon Street. Pleasure boating on Lake Pontchartrain. Shrimp boats coming in with tons of marijuana. Stately mansions in the Garden District. Shadows of muggers making a play for your purse under Jackson Square lamplight.

To paraphrase a line in the movie The Big Easy, *the police are the only ones standing between us and them, darlin'. And Dexter Accardo is an officer of more than twenty years. With long legs poured into blue jeans, punctuated by a big silver buckle, and a conservative haircut that probably hasn't changed since he joined the Jefferson Parish sheriff's office, Dexter looks very much like the college kid he once was.*

Although he was always attracted to the notion of police work, he was just a college boy doing a summer job when he happened to notice something odd. And then his calling unfurled before him like a long, straight road through the Louisiana bayous.

I had wanted to be a policeman since I was in high school. It had all the elements that made me happy. It had a lot of excitement attached to it, but it was also a chance to get involved in the community. I like people, and I like being around them.

Of course, everyone likes the intrigue of running after people and chasing down bad guys. But it's not like that all the time. It can be just as rewarding helping a lady with a flat tire. This work simply turns the course of what's going wrong.

While I was in college I started working in the local shipyard that was building navy destroyers at the time. This shipyard had the largest number of employees in the state and was really interesting. I was just doing miscellaneous office work, but I got to go out and see all walks of life at the shipyard—people from the bayous and from the city. And I was naive about everything.

I had graduated from high school in 1969, and while there probably were drugs out there, I didn't know anything about them. I was on another planet. I raced cars and chased girls.

So the shipyard was my first involvement with people into drugs—the big things were marijuana and LSD. I went up to the shipyard's vice president and told him there was all this dealing going on, and he said, "Really? Can you get any of those drugs? Here's ten dollars, go see if you can buy some drugs off the shipyard." He was pro–law enforcement, but he was also concerned about people doing drugs and dropping steel plates on people's heads.

I bought a bag of marijuana, and the next thing I knew,

the sheriff was asking me if I'd be willing to work under-cover. In life things fall into place.

I started earning a double salary. The shipyard paid me, and the police department paid me. I had money stashed in shoe boxes. I was living at home and never told my parents about it.

But I was basically on my own. The narcotics division that hired me had jurisdiction over twelve or thirteen parishes. So I could go anywhere, which they liked, because the shipyard was a melting pot, and I could go all over southern Louisiana making buys. I could go any-where, and no one knew where I was. Not even the police department.

I look back now and think, Boy, was I dumb. Once I went on a deal to buy some marijuana, and we had to go by boat for a half hour through the bayou. We went out to this camp where there's these guys with long hair—you have to realize I've never had long hair. They were real weirdos, spaced out, and with guns. It wasn't fashionable in those days to be a narc, and they kept saying, "I wish I knew where one was. I'd take him out and chop him up, and they'd never find him." And there I was, trying to look innocent.

Today the drug dealers are more educated, and you re-ally have to do your homework. But somehow I always landed on my feet. I was young and goofy, and I think that saved me. But I also feel that when it's your turn to go, it's your turn to go.

After that operation, they pulled me up from under-cover. So I went to the police academy and, after graduation, eventually rejoined narcotics. Vice, intelligence, and narcotics were the elite of the police department.

Being surrounded by the drug scene, Dexter could easily have succumbed to the lure of narcotics, as some officers do all over the country. But focus, quick wits, and priorities kept him from even trying the stuff.

I spent almost twelve years in narcotics, and I probably only know a couple of police officers who did drugs. And they were ultimately arrested, either by me or someone else. People always ask me if I ever used drugs, but I never have. I've never been tempted to step over the line. My job was so precious to me, why would I want to jeopardize my job for something that was illegal and for which I had no desire? My only desire was my job.

Undercover work is unique because you always have to be one step ahead of the dealers. A true dealer wants you to sample his product for two reasons. One, to demonstrate the quality of his produce and, two, to make sure you're not a policeman. I'd find ways of getting around that, like showing up a half hour late and saying, "Just give me the stuff and let me get out of here. I gotta get going, I've got something to do."

The strongest thing I've taken is Excedrin. And I do take Tagemet for indigestion, strictly Wal-Mart over-the-counter. I've never had to say I'm going to surrender my strength to alcohol or pills. At the same time, I have sympathy for people in law enforcement who get addicted to prescription drugs for things like back injuries. It's easier to take a pill for back pain and make it go away.

I did the majority of my drinking while I was in narcotics, because we'd work until midnight and then drink until six in the morning, just to unwind, and cut up, and chase women.

One good thing about being in narcotics is that you get to meet a lot of nice women. If you regularly went to certain clubs, they knew who you were. There was a little arrow on me that said, "This guy is straight." You were either a drug user or not a drug user. Most women don't want to mess with no jackasses.

But there was plenty of action in those days. Kicking doors, chasing people, high-speed chases. That was fun. Those were really great times.

Not everything was great, though. Dexter was surrounded by his first wife's family members, who were certain he'd never amount to much of anything. And there were criminals who wanted to make certain he'd not live to see the next day. If this were a Hollywood script, these moments would put him in an identity crisis. They only served to remind and convince him that he was indeed a police officer.

I was in a shoot-out, and the officer who was with me got killed. We had graduated from high school together. A guy hiding in a dark living room had the option to shoot me or him. But he shot him. Clipped his aorta, and he was dead before he hit the floor.

It took me a long time to get over that. It was one of the few occasions when I had the rage. I wanted to shoot someone. But I was still committed to the work. If we got a good drug dealer, what did that mean? It meant that maybe your kids wouldn't get drugs.

And the main temptation to lure him away from police work only backfired.

My first wife was from a wealthy family. Her mom and dad thought nothing bad about the police, but they always thought I would never amount to anything. They owned a bar— Well, they owned many other things, but there was this bar. I'll never forget one day I was sitting at the kitchen table at their house, and they said, "We want to make you an offer. Quit the police department tomorrow, and we'll give you the bar—outright."

I said, "I don't want to be no bar owner." And they said, "You stupid ass. Look at this home. How do you think we got this home and everything in it? From that bar. Paid for. Cash."

I had only one answer for him: no. I didn't get mad. I didn't get confused. I just said no.

That didn't go over too big. A year passes. I had been operating some heavy equipment to make money on the side, but I couldn't buy my own equipment. So my father-in-law buys some equipment. Back at the table, he says, "I've got a proposal. I'll give you all the equipment and get you in the operating engineers' union where you can work in the refineries and make beaucoup money. It will cost me an extra $5,000 but I'll get you in. Quit the police department."

My ex-wife could never release herself from her parents. I just couldn't be married to her and her mother and father. So I left. I don't need no ultimatums. Money is great, but only if you enjoy making it.

How could I choose not to be a police officer? I can't even imagine that. You'd be asking me to choose to be something I'm not. Sure, my ex-wife's family has a lot of money, and I could be living in a bigger house today. But there's nothing I want now that I can't buy myself on the money I'm making on my own. And one thing's for sure: you can't buy happiness in your job.

There was no way my father-in-law could get me to quit

the department. I can't even say I was tempted. More like I was amazed that he would have the guts to try again.

He used the wrong thing to tempt me away from the police department—money. What could tempt me? Nothing. Nothing at all. Not even another police department, probably.

He's now trying to offer my son some kind of deal involving a hotel. In all these years I thought he would have changed. But he hasn't changed one iota. My son doesn't ask for anything. If he looks at it as an investment, something down the road, but still seeks to choose his career, that's his business. But I think he's going to tell his grandfather to take it up the street, just like I did twenty years ago.

So Dexter stubbornly stuck to police work, where he would develop a valuable network of friends who could continue to work with him throughout his career.

A man's only as good as his contacts.

Being in narcotics, I had connections all over the United States. Because I did drug cases all over, I had the ability now to pick up the phone and talk with someone from, say, Los Angeles or New York. While I was in narcotics we would have people we would try and try and try to get. But if they are highfalutin people with money and political clout, we could never get them.

So we'd let their ass get on a plane to, say, L.A., call our friends in L.A., and they would get them at the airport. Nothing's better than picking up the phone and saying, "Hey, Joe, look, can you do this for me?"

And of course I would always reciprocate, too. I've got a rapport all over the country.

But so do the bad guys. Dexter's narcotics work would eventually take him around the country—in fact, around the world—to places where a stranger standing casually next to him could easily be the one to finish his career, if not his life.

I went to Miami one time and met a guy in Little Havana, which I didn't know beans about. Earlier I had busted him, and now he had become an informant. He was a Cuban refugee, and his family was very wealthy, with plenty of connections. So we were meeting on business. At one point he leaned over and whispered, "You know, I could have had you killed right here."

Part of staying alive is just waking up and realizing that the criminal knows all about you. Criminals are as good at profiling police officers as police officers are good at profiling the criminals.

The number-one day for drug smuggling is Sunday, because that's when a lot of the detectives are off. On Super Bowl Sunday? That was a big day for shrimp boats to come in with a load of weed. Because they know all us policemen like to watch the Super Bowl.

We were profiling them. They were profiling us.

I also got to go to the Golden Triangle, where Burma, Laos, and Thailand meet. They don't waste one square foot of mud there. Growing poppies is part of their culture. The U.S. government has a deal where it spends millions and millions of dollars over there for drug interdiction. But the local governments take their share. They've done it for hundreds and hundreds of years. You will not change those people's culture. It will never stop. All we can do is become a little wiser as to their ways of import and export.

And motivation. You've got a guy who gets so much money for such a little crop. If it wasn't illegal he wouldn't get anything.

Narcotics is a young officer's division. And time and age eventually caught up with Dexter. He was due to find a new line of work—within, of course, the police department. With all his contacts nationwide, learning a new field wasn't going to be tough. All the answers he needed were just a phone call away.

Eventually I had done everything I could humanly do, and I was too old for narcotics work. At thirty-six I couldn't run so quickly anymore. So I would let the younger policemen chase them, and I would drive my car and let them run to me.

But the last thing I would ever want to do is be brain-dead. As much as I loved the work, I knew when it was time to move on. I missed narcotics and was a little distraught for a while. I had left the biggest part of my life there. But then I took over the special operations section. They call it LASER: land, air, sea emergency rescue. I took over a division I knew nothing about, which was really good.

When I took it over in January 1986, it encompassed the mounted division. I didn't know anything about horses other than the fact they eat a lot and they shit a lot. They wore more shoes than me and you combined. Rubber shoes to metal shoes, depending on their application. And they cost a lot of money.

And I had to learn about the K-9 division. I knew nothing about dogs, other than they'll bite the hell out of you. I had to learn about the application of a police dog and how put him on the street as a tool. I ended up buying the best dogs I could find—in Germany. And I hired the best K-9 trainer in the state.

I also had the search-and-rescue side, and all their equipment was raggedy. So I went out and got all new equipment—new boats and everything. The sheriff was always supportive of everything I wanted.

It was more than just buying equipment. I also had to learn about search and rescue, about how people drown, so we can find them later—if, of course, we don't find them before they drown. Where you drown is where you stay. You go down there and stay until your body fills with gas. Then you come up and float out to sea.

I had people working for me who knew more about the field than I did. And that was a good thing. But I also went to outside sources for information. I needed to see what my staff was saying versus what the real world was saying.

You can tell me anything you want, and I'll listen to you. But I'll get to the bottom of it one way or another, the truth of the way it should be done. So I went to other law enforcement agencies. No matter what I needed to know, I just had to pick up the phone, call a buddy in New York or L.A., and say, "Hey, who do you know who's expert in this?"

Along with LASER, Dexter also handled the bomb squad, where he stays today. He is now handling a team of technicians who responded to over one hundred calls in 1995 and disposed of forty-three bombs. So it was back to school for Dexter.

Sure is a bitch to command something that you don't know anything about. So I put in an application to go to bomb school. Every two years we go back and get recertified. You've got to keep your mind refueled. Sitting around pushing papers doesn't make any sense.

Every once in a while I hear someone say TGIF. What is that? Don't know nothing about it. Fridays don't exist, because every day is a good day. Time just flies too quick for me. I always kid my guys that there are too many damn holidays, too many off days. In twenty-two years I've missed one or two days sick. It's not that I haven't been sick. It's just that if I'm going to be sick, I'd just as soon be sick in the office than be sick and be even more miserable at home.

The only meaning of time is to make appointments. I'm the four-hour-sleep kind of guy. Life's too short, why sleep it away?

I've had such a good life. I hope I can live to be a hundred.

17

Inherit Your Calling

*This is hard work; sometimes I wonder why
I'm doing it. But when I get a doctor's report that the
antivenin saved a child's life, then it's all worth it.*

MARILYN BLOOM

52, The Scorpion Lady

Sometimes it feels as if our work is nothing at all like what we thought it would be, that somehow we've settled for plan B. The tasks we're handed don't quite match up with the grander accomplishments we know we could achieve. Instead, we're stuck carrying out someone else's vision.

While filling another's shoes can be a lot harder and feel less satisfying than creating your own dream, the reality is that your calling may be to pick up the work left off by someone before you. That doesn't make what you do any less valuable. It just means that there's a lot of work to go around on this planet, and your contribution, whether newly created or inherited, is vital to its well-being.

In her windowless basement office and lab, Marilyn Bloom is hard at work, growing bacteria, fungi, and algae. This microbial material will be used by students at Arizona State University in their lab experiments. "It's almost impossible to teach classes if you don't have living material to work with," she explains.

A pretty woman with a ready smile, she travels the polished corridors of her subterranean world, pausing at the walk-in, temperature- and light-controlled room to check the test tubes and petri dishes full of cultures that, to the outsider, look like green swamp goo. In her office, amid the microscopes, Bunsen burners, and centrifuge equipment, are symbols of the most unusual aspect of Marilyn's work—posters of scorpions, scorpion skeletons of all sizes, and every scorpion knickknack imaginable. On her desk is an aquarium that is home to a couple of live scorpions—asleep for the time being under a rock. There is no doubt that this is where the Scorpion Lady works.

Marilyn doesn't spend all of her working hours in the basement. She's frequently at ASU's hot and dusty farm. With the help of a goat wrangler, she injects tiny amounts of scorpion venom in her goats, then draws blood from them after their immune systems have produced antibodies to the venom.

Marilyn Bloom is one of only a handful of people in the world who produce scorpion antivenin. Thirteen years ago the project was dropped in her lap as a temporary assignment. Or so she thought. Little did she know the impact her newest challenge would have on her life and the lives of countless others.

In the 1950s, Dr. Herbert Stahnke, who was the poisonous animals guru of the world at the time, discovered that more people were dying from scorpion stings than from rattlesnake bites. Rattlesnake antivenin was already close to being commercially available, and so he developed and began producing the scorpion antivenin here at ASU.

When the person running the scorpion antivenin production lab retired, the department asked me to take it on temporarily. Before coming to ASU, I had worked in doctors' offices for several years and knew how to give people shots. I guess the department figured that meant I could stick needles into goats!

It was supposed to be for just a couple of years until new faculty came in, but when they did, no one wanted to touch the antivenin project with a ten-foot pole. You see, the project takes a lot of time, so none of the faculty was interested in pursuing it. And because providing scorpion antivenin is basically a public service, faculty members don't get the brownie points they need for promotion and tenure. It's the "publish or perish" syndrome. Since I'm staff, not faculty, I don't have to worry about that.

This is hard work; sometimes I wonder why I'm doing it. It's so hot in Arizona during the summer, trying to round up and draw blood from the goats with the all the flies and heat. And in the winter, it's freezing and your hands get so cold you can barely manipulate the equipment. But when I get a doctor's report that the antivenin saved a child's life, then it's all worth it.

Marilyn keeps records on how the antivenin is used and its results. She is regularly in touch with doctors' offices, clinics, and hospitals all over the country. The title of Scorpion Lady was bestowed on her long ago; to this day she's matter-of-fact about her celebrity and unique job description.

I don't know how I gained celebrity as the Scorpion Lady. I guess it's an exotic news story. But I was already getting media coverage for growing bacteria, fungi, and algae. People thought that that was a strange way to make a living!

The reason this facility is the only one in the country that produces scorpion antivenin is because Arizona has the only significant population of a potentially medically important scorpion. Our problematic scorpion is a Sonoran desert critter—*Centruroides sculpturatus*, the bark scorpion. This tiny straw-colored animal had its beginning in Mexico and managed to migrate north. Phoenix is the only major metropolitan area that has any great accumulation of them.

A medically important scorpion is one that could send you or me to the hospital, but one that could kill a child. The good news is we haven't had a single human death from a scorpion sting in this country in thirty years, partly because of the antivenin and also because the medical community has learned to recognize a scorpion sting and treat it. Whereas in Mexico, as many as a thousand people, mostly small children, die each year from scorpion stings, mainly because they lack quick access to medical facilities.

Marilyn says that despite its potentially lethal sting, the scorpion doesn't deserve its evil reputation.

Throughout time, scorpions have been portrayed in a negative light. Even paintings of Roman soldiers taking Christ up to the Cross portrayed scorpions on their robes.

Scorpions have been around for over 450 million years in all parts of the world. They didn't use to be in New Zealand or the British Isles, but of course "homo stupidus"—man—in his journeys took them along, probably unwittingly.

Scorpions can go a year without eating. They can withstand radiation 200 times greater than humans can stand, and they can go without water for three to four months.

In the winter, the only things that can kill them are successive hard freezes (en masse). Freezing them once won't do it. You could put a scorpion in your freezer for a couple of days, take it out and put it on the table to thaw, and within a few hours it'd be walking off.

Who do you think will rule the world when we humans are gone? Scorpions, cockroaches, and rats!

When describing how the venom is collected, Marilyn's eyes light up and her voice rises with emotion. She clearly loves to tell this story.

First, I contact the provider of the venom. He has the tricky part—he and his daughter hunt and collect the scorpions, then milk them. You have to handle scorpions carefully. You could spray half a can of Raid on them and they'd walk away, but if you poke a little hole in their exoskeleton, they'll die very quickly.

Next, they electrically stimulate the tail so that a little drop of venom will appear on the tip of the stinger. This is how it's done. They wear rubber gloves with double material on the fingers, grab the animal to leave the tail free, then with the other hand take a pair of forceps that are wired and run it up the tail. There's a foot control for the electricity.

They work with a pan full of writhing scorpions and an empty pan for the ones that have been milked. Pick one up, do it, set it down. The daughter can sometimes do five hundred in an hour. The venom is collected with a small pipette and placed into a serum vial, then freeze-dried.

I buy the venom, mix it here, put it in a syringe, and inject my goats. What I do causes the toxin to release slowly, so it stimulates the goats' immune system. A new goat takes about three months to get its antibodies up to a therapeutic level. With goats I've used before, I can get them up in five weeks.

Marilyn says that, historically, horses have been used for all antivenin serums. But around 25 percent of the population is allergic to horse serum. Every year a few people die because of receiving an injection containing horse serum.

Drawing blood from my goats is not uncomfortable for them, and I use the same type of needles that are used in the hospital or doctor's office. The goats give us a lot more trouble when we try to trim their toenails! They're happy to see me because I have sugar cubes for them. Each goat does have its own personality—some are ornery, others stand reasonably still because they're more interested in getting their sugar.

After I draw the blood every week over the course of several weeks, I let it clot, then spin it down to get rid of all the cellular components. The amber-colored serum that's left contains the potent antibodies to the venom. It's then filter-sterilized, bottled, and frozen, ready to go.

How this life-saving serum is produced does have its drawbacks, a kind of Catch-22 situation with the federal government—with Marilyn caught in the middle.

I have to do sterility and safety testing each time I produce a batch of scorpion antivenin. That costs money, but if I don't do it, the federal government will shut me down. Also, I can't do the bottling here; I have to use an FDA-approved laboratory. But I can't do it there because you can't put a non-FDA-approved drug in an FDA-approved area!

Since we're non-FDA-approved, I'm not allowed to send the serum out of state. But since Arizona has the significant scorpion population, so far it doesn't seem to be a problem. Although now there may be a problem, with the bark scorpion making it up to Las Vegas when palm trees from this area were planted during the construction of new hotels and resorts. I also got a call from a Colorado emergency room about a man who was stung while unloading boxes from a commercial truck. Unfortunately, he proceeded to beat the scorpion to a pulp, so I wasn't able to identify the species. (The man lived.)

It would be helpful to be FDA-approved, but it would

take a long time and the university isn't interested in doing that. It's probably the "if it ain't broke, don't fix it" attitude.

With no reliable financial support and with plenty of demand, Marilyn has learned over the years to trust her instincts about how best to run and finance the project she inherited.

There's also no direct line in the budget for what I do; there's no equipment. I'm left to my own devices to find money for funding.

One of my biggest contributors is a British citizen who, years ago, bought a tract of land in Mexico. He and savings-and-loan mogul Charles Keating Jr. were talking about providing Mexico with scorpion antivenin (this was when Keating was still in the good graces of the people of Arizona, before the S&L scandals). Keating's staff approached me about it, but when Keating ended up in prison, the talks stopped. I sent some of the antivenin anyway. It turned out that the British citizen's eighteen-month-old son had been stung and needed the antivenin. Well, now I can have anything I want. The last check he sent was for $10,000.

I don't need a lot of money to run the project: food for the goats, and materials to bleed them and process the serum.

Growing cultures, wrestling goats, and fielding out-of-state calls from emergency rooms about scorpion stings was not how Marilyn envisioned her future when she was a young girl growing up in Wisconsin. She wanted to be a singer and have a career in the entertainment field.

Music was my first love. I would've been a performer, but I tried it and decided it wasn't for me. I had won a beauty contest, and I did some professional singing, but I didn't like the people I had to deal with.

I also flunked music theory in school. I needed a science class to graduate, so somewhere along the line I picked up a couple of science classes and got A's. So I switched to the sciences.

Everyone wanted me to go to college, and I was determined to get a degree. My aunt had left me money for my education, but by this time I was married, and my husband and I used it instead to buy a house. My husband promised my mother that he would help me finish my education, which he did. He left me for another woman a year later, but hc kcpt his bargain!

After graduating, I went to work at a doctor's office—I had two children to raise and no child support.

One of the professors at ASU was my undergraduate adviser and headed the committee to find someone for the culture curator position. I had had classes with three of the professors on the committee. One of them called me and told me to apply for the position. Six weeks later I was offered the job.

I had been at ASU a year or two and started taking classes—years ago you could take a class for five dollars. One of the professors needed an extra hand on a research project, so I helped him, and my name was included on the paper. Then I gave an oral presentation on the project at a local branch meeting. I discovered I liked public speaking! So I told other faculty members that I would volunteer on research projects. By this time I was taking classes beyond the bachelor's degree level, and one of the faculty suggested that I go for my master's.

Pretty soon I had a program of study laid out and a research project dropped in my lap—it was a real boost to my self-esteem. Motherhood was still very important to me, but the older my kids got, the less they needed me. After being a single parent and trying to be everything to everybody, I decided that I couldn't do that anymore and survive. My attitude now is I do the best I can with what I have to work with.

Marilyn has always wanted her life and work to have meaning, to be able to say she made a difference. The scorpion antivenin project was a "surprise" calling. Talking to schoolchildren about general biology is yet another vocation that has grown out of her love of the sciences and her childhood dream of being a performer.

I talk to around two thousand schoolchildren every year. I take along my skull and insect collections and live snake. And I love to talk to at-risk kids, especially Native American children. The elders on the reservation want the children steeped in the Native American tradition, which I agree is important, because knowing where they came from gives them a sense of their own personal being. But if they want to go on for further education after high school, they need to leave the reservation.

Then they can return to help their community. It's much easier for the people in the community to accept education and guidance from one of their own than from an outsider. If one of my kids came up to me ten years from now and told me that he had been thinking of dropping out of school until I talked to his class, but then stayed, that would make me feel wonderful—that I had made a difference.

18

Find the Right Fit

*I was living a selfish life. I liken it to a
rainbow—it looked nice from the outside, but it was
vapor. There was no substance to my life because
I wasn't doing anything for anyone else. ·*

JAMES MCCLOSKEY

54, Executive Director, Centurion Ministries, Inc.

No one wants to be an outsider. It just doesn't feel right. And trying to fit in, when you know you can't, invites disaster, for you and everyone around you.

The truth is, when you're in the wrong place—whether it's a job, a relationship, or a location—everything else feels wrong, too. But take heart. Being a fish out of water can be a lifesaving opportunity for you to ask yourself: Why am I so unhappy? What can I learn from this? Be still and listen for the answers deep inside you. That's where you'll find your calling.

Jim McCloskey is a buoyant, gregarious man. Gesturing with his hands to drive home a point, he is at turns both passionate and pissed off. But never reticent.

This man of the cloth has a huge bone to pick with the American criminal justice system. Witnesses who lie. Police who are pressured to wrap up the case. Prosecutors who focus only on evidence that supports a preconceived theory. Any one of these factors can result in a wrongful conviction, and an innocent man or woman sitting in prison for life or on death row.

For Jim McCloskey, that kind of injustice is worth fighting. When not on the road meeting with clients in prison and doing exhaustive investigations, he strategizes with his staff in a modest office in the well-heeled community of Princeton, New Jersey. There they pore over detailed reports on cases Centurion Ministries has yet to accept. Clients fall into one category: "You have to be serving life or on death row, with no appeals left. You're simply dead in the water," Jim says.

On the walls is a photo gallery chronicling Centurion's work over the years: convicts and their families standing on the prison steps on the day of their release, a framed cover of Time *magazine depicting death-row inmate Roger Coleman, days before his execution, a sentence Jim couldn't stop despite the evidence he uncovered pointing to Roger's innocence.*

The ministry's outer office, a war room of sorts, is lined with desks and computers—some new, mostly old—and bookshelves where equally distributed among the reference and law books are bestselling paperbacks about America's more sensational crimes. In full view is a board listing Centurion's active cases, both men and women on death row and serving life imprisonment, and their status. Currently, there are fifteen names on the board.

Jim McCloskey's work seems worlds away from the affluent lifestyle he once enjoyed on Philadelphia's Main Line.

My father was the executive vice-president of Mc-Closkey & Co., a large, family-owned construction firm that built one of the congressional office buildings and RFK Stadium in Washington, D.C. My uncle, Matt Mc-Closkey, who founded the company, was a bigwig in the Democratic Party and the U.S. ambassador to Ireland.

I was raised in a conservative Presbyterian family. Every Sunday we went to church—service in the morning, then back again at night for more. It was too much. Not that I didn't like church—I met a lot of friends there—but six hours every week!

In high school I saw a short film about the night life in

Tokyo with all the neon signs and women in kimonos going into nightclubs. I thought to myself, "This is exciting; I want to do this." (I had a romantic image of myself as a man of the world.) My dream was to be an international businessman in Japan.

Before going about making his dream come true, Jim took a slight detour after college—the navy. He requested shore duty in Japan as his first assignment, and got it.

So here I am in Japan in my bright white ensign uniform. My dream fulfilled! There was no doubt in my mind that I would return as a businessman once I got out of the service. But first I volunteered for Vietnam. I wanted to be where the action was. Again, I applied for the assignment, and within three weeks I was issued orders.

I served in the Mekong Delta as an adviser to the South Vietnamese Junk Force patrolling the rivers. I lived on a Vietnamese base with the Vietnamese and only one other American.

After my tour was over, I went to the American Graduate School for International Management in Phoenix to get a master's in foreign trade. One of my professors, who knew I wanted to go to Japan, gave me names of people over there who might hire me. I packed my bags, borrowed $1,200 from my parents, and flew to Tokyo with no job offers.

I wasn't scared. I've always had this faith that the adventure would yield what I had imagined.

Within three weeks I had a job with a small company, a market research management consulting firm. We helped Western companies that wanted to do business in Japan by doing marketing studies and helping to negotiate joint-venture agreements with Japanese companies. It was just the kind of work I had hoped to be able to get.

But after four years of life in Japan, something began to well up in Jim, a sense of not belonging, of being out of place. Always a "take action" type, he changed his environment when it no longer worked for him.

Over time I became disillusioned with being an American expatriate in Tokyo. You see, back then any person living there was known as a *gaijin,* an outside person. The Japanese were a very enclosed people and culture.

So I came home to Philadelphia and began working for a well-known consulting firm. My mission was to build the firm's business with Japanese companies in the United States and then establish our own business in Japan. I was in my mid-thirties, made good money, owned a house on Philadelphia's Main Line, drove a Lincoln Continental— had all the accoutrements.

And I felt empty. I was living a selfish life. I liken it to a rainbow—it looked nice from the outside, but it was vapor.

There was no substance to my life because I wasn't doing anything for anyone else. I was just out there with no mission, no focus—just total insignificance.

Also, there was a deeper dimension to my emptiness that I knew was spiritual. So I started going back to church (I had told my parents when I was a freshman in college that I was never going to church again). I looked at the pastor every week touching the lives of other people—he became a role model for me. I couldn't wait for Sundays to roll around! I thought, He's living life. He's doing things for others; he's touching their hearts and souls. What am I doing? I'm making money for a few wealthy business partners. That's when I began to see what I was doing as a sham, and the only caring that took place was that of turning over as many clients as possible and making money.

At night I would read the Scriptures and the New Testament. The passage that got to me was when Christ said to the disciples, "Follow me and I will make you fishers of men." That's what I wanted to be—a strong catalyst in helping people change their lives.

It really started to eat away at me—is God calling me into the ministry? To leave everything and go follow Christ?

As Jim drew closer to defining his calling, he felt less engaged in his chosen career and increasingly distanced from his surroundings.

I couldn't tell anyone about it. People would just say, "You're crazy," and give you all the pat conventional wisdom in the world that doesn't have anything to do with the reality of your internal being. I didn't even tell my minister until the last few months when it really grabbed me by the throat that I should leave the business world.

I prayed, thought, agonized. The last two years in particular were difficult because I felt I had one foot in one camp and one foot in the other. My heart was with the church and Christ, but I was still very much a man of the world. But the closer I came to being called, the less interested I was in what was going on at work.

Then it happened. I was home alone on a Saturday night, really wrestling with this whole proposition of starting a new life. I was reading the Scriptures and came across the last chapter in the gospel of John, where the resurrected Christ says to Peter, "When you were young, you walked where you would. When you are older, another will gird you and take you where perhaps you do not want to go." I thought Christ was talking directly to me. Suddenly the two years of agonizing were over, and I said, "I'm yours; I surrender everything, and I will follow you."

It was an enlightenment and a lifting of my worries. There were no angels, no voices—just the internal realization that this was my purpose. On Monday morning I told my boss that I had decided to go into the ministry. He said, "Jim, I didn't even know you went to church!"

He was shocked and stunned, like everyone else—they thought I had lost my marbles. My mother told me, "If the ministry will make you happy, then fine. But you will never be a church minister." She didn't think I would have the patience to be a church minister, that that just wasn't me.

My boss convinced me that I should stay one more year to finish up the work we had started on opening up business in Japan. I knew that my work there wasn't complete, so I readily agreed.

But when the year was up, the head of the firm called me into his office to talk to me about "this ministry thing." He wanted me to put off going to the seminary for another couple of years and offered to pay me $100,000 a year plus living expenses if I would go to Tokyo and start up the company's office there.

I didn't have to give it a second thought. I said, "Sorry, but it's off to the seminary I go."

School was scary for me at first because I never was much of a student. And dorm life was rough after having my own home and privacy. But I never had one scintilla of a doubt, ever! I believed it was a call, that I was picked out to do this work.

Jim's unwavering belief that he had found the perfect fit for his life's work was about to be tested by someone who had only one thing in common with Jim—he, too, knew what it felt like to be a fish out of water.

During the second year of seminary, students have to do fieldwork. I chose to be a student chaplain at Trenton State Prison, mainly because I was curious to meet the prisoners and see the inside of a prison.

I was assigned to two tiers with forty guys and could go from cell to cell. Two of the forty men kept telling me they were innocent. One of them was an illiterate junkie from the streets of Newark—George "Chiefie" de Los Santos.

I had been warned not to get involved in the prisoners' cases or do anything on the outside for them. And I was told that all prisoners say they're innocent—which isn't true, by the way—but that was all Chiefie talked about during our visits.

Chiefie was in his sixth year of a life sentence for killing a used-car salesman in Newark. Even the other inmates on his tier were telling me he was innocent! I promised him I would read his trial transcripts over the Thanksgiving holiday. I knew it was forbidden, but I felt I had to do it for him anyway. I read them carefully, and it all boiled down to his word against that of the prosecution's main witness, who told the jury that he was in county jail with de Los Santos when de Los Santos confessed to him.

Now, I knew nothing about the criminal justice system; I'd never even served on a jury. So I started to have doubts about Chiefie's innocence. I asked him why I should believe him. He explained to me that the witness was a junkie like him who was also a snitch and constantly in trouble with the law.

The dilemma Jim faced seemed overwhelming: should he help this convicted criminal, who might not be telling the truth, and defy the seminary, risking his own vocation?

For me, it came down to who are you going to believe? I believed Chiefie. That's when I decided to take a full year off from school to devote to his case. Mind you, I've just left the business world to become a minister. Now I'm taking time off to work for a junkie convicted of murder. Who am I going to discuss *this* with? I didn't even talk to my minister this time.

I knew it wasn't enough to go back to the dorm and pray for him; I needed to help him. And I felt that God was opening this door for me. For the first time, I felt that this was what I was meant to do in my life, to free innocent people from prison. It filled me with a sense of purpose and mission. And if I saved Chiefie's life, I would be saving my own. I wouldn't just be giving, I would be receiving. (You know, my mother turned out to be right when she said I would never be a church minister!)

Well, I didn't know what to do next, but I was a grown man with world experience and common sense. I'm sure I relied on the skills I had developed as a businessman, although not consciously. The first thing I did was to move into the home of an elderly woman, where I had a rent-free room in exchange for doing errands for her.

Since I had my own savings to do the work, I investigated the case myself, actually becoming a gumshoe and looking for the main witness in Chiefie's trial. I formed a defense committee composed of members of the Presbyterian church in New Jersey and raised $25,000 to hire a lawyer.

In my investigation I discovered that the witness had done the exact same thing to his cousin when he was on trial for murder. The cousin was also at Trenton State Prison and must have figured that if I could get Chiefie off, I could get him off, too. So he helped me meet his family in Newark, and through them I found and met the witness. Over time, he admitted to me that he had lied.

I was so naive that when I went to the prosecutor's office, I thought he would be moved by what we had uncovered. Instead, he kicked me out of his office! He didn't want to hear that he had wrongly prosecuted a criminal.

Our lawyer presented the new evidence to the judge at an evidentiary hearing, and the judge freed Chiefie. It was two and a half years since I had first read his trial transcripts.

Helping an innocent man find freedom brought into focus for Jim what form his calling should take—to seek justice for the innocent in prison.

By this time, I had already returned to finish school and was still visiting prisoners. I met two other inmates at Trenton State Prison whose innocence I believed in. I told them I didn't know what I could do for them, that I had to become a minister and didn't have any more money for this kind of work.

But then two things happened. First, my parents came into an extraordinary gain in income and gave each of their children $10,000 as a tax-free gift. I thought maybe it was a sign from God that this was my seed money. That same week I had a dream that sealed the deal for me. In the dream I was back in Vietnam standing on a riverbank with a friend. A boat appeared full of refugees clinging to every possible space. Suddenly the entire boat sank. I said to my friend, "This is terrible that all these people have drowned and there's nothing we can do about it." Suddenly out of nowhere helicopters came and dropped Navy SEALs into the water. They started bringing up all these people and they're alive!

The dream meant to me that I should go back into the

prisons because those people are as good as dead—and even though others might think there is nothing that can save them, I can.

I told the two inmates that I would be doing this work full-time from now on. I incorporated my ministry as a non-profit organization and then went to work on their cases.

The name for Jim's ministry came to him in the car one day on the way to prison. He was thinking about the centurion at the foot of the cross who looked up at Christ and said, "Surely this one was innocent." The name Centurion Ministries was born.

For the next six years Centurion Ministries was just me, living and working out of a rent-free room. I had two lawyers who, even though I couldn't pay them much, took the cases because they believed in the work I was doing.

When we freed our third inmate, Centurion Ministries started getting widespread media coverage. Before, I was raising and spending about $30,000 a year. With national exposure, everything changed.

Suddenly we had credibility, and then the contributions started coming in. Finally I could hire a full-time associate, Kate Hill. She had read about the ministry and also felt a calling to this work.

Requests for help from inmates and their families poured in from all over the country. And then we received pleas for help from death row.

Jimmy Wingo was on death row at Angola Prison in Louisiana. Clarence Brandley was sitting on death row in Texas. Both were scheduled to die very soon. I thought, Are things getting out of control here? I was secure working in New Jersey, but now I'm looking at death-row cases in the South. That's a whole 'nother world.

But I went ahead and met with the two inmates and their lawyers. After hearing Brandley's story, I told his lawyers I would take his case, but needed a car and a place to stay. For six weeks I lived in the garage of one attorney's home, and the other let me use his mother's car.

A lot happened in those six weeks during my investigation. I met with a witness who admitted to me that he had given false testimony during Brandley's trial.

Why people feel compelled to confess to Jim is still a mystery to him, although he believes that almost everyone wants to tell the truth, particularly to someone they see as God's personal representative here on earth.

I'm not sure why people confess to me. I do know that I approach them with respect, no matter who they are or what they've done. I treat them the way I would like to be treated. Over time, we develop a rapport and trust, and they come to know I'm serious and genuine. Slowly but surely they feel they can tell me things they haven't told other people. It just starts coming out.

In Brandley's case, once we brought the witness forward, Clarence was freed. But it didn't work out that way for Jimmy Wingo. The two main trial witnesses against Mr. Wingo admitted on videotape that they were coerced into lying at the trial by a deputy sheriff. I personally presented our evidence to the Louisiana Board of Pardons the day before the execution, but they weren't interested in hearing it, and Jimmy was executed on June 16, 1987.

I was with Jimmy until a half hour before his execution. He thanked me for all I did and encouraged me to work for all the other Wingos of the world. He was courageous and had a quiet kind of dignity and grace.

After the execution, the Baton Rouge newspaper ran this headline: "McCloskey's First Failure." It wasn't my failure; it was the failure of the criminal justice system to at least consider our evidence.

Another death-row inmate, Roger Coleman, who was executed in Virginia despite evidence showing who the real killers were, behaved much the same way at the end as Jimmy Wingo. As they were strapped in their respective electric chairs, their last words were practically the same: I am innocent and I am being executed wrongly, but I forgive those who have done this.

Those two uneducated rural men taught me how to die. We all know we're going to die someday, but not how or when. They knew. And the way they met that unjust fate with equanimity of spirit was amazing.

For a long time Jim could feel only anger over the executions. They shook his faith in God before finally deepening it again and his resolve to show others how innocent people in this country are convicted and executed.

Until Wingo's execution, I always believed that somehow the truth would prevail. When I made the presentation before the Louisiana Board of Pardons the day before Jimmy's execution, the chairman wasn't even there. I found out later that the reason was because he was being indicted and later pled guilty to selling pardons to convicts!

I kept asking, "Where are you, God? Why do you allow innocent people to get executed?" There was a period of time when I separated from God. I continued my work, but began to lose my faith in the existence of God. It left me feeling spiritually drained and empty.

The only answer that ever came was in the Scriptures when God talks about loving your enemies and says that it rains on the just and the unjust, and the sun shines on the evil and the good.

Coming to terms with the reality that bad things happen to good people helped Jim understand how crucial his ministry had become to those who truly had no place else to turn.

So far, Centurion has freed seventeen people. To me,

they're miracles, because with each case you face unbelievable odds. We receive close to a thousand new requests for
help every year, and we document and respond to each
one. But because of the research that goes into each re-
quest before we can take on a new case, sometimes years
go by. These people have to be persistent. I call it the persistence of innocence.

*That persistence also rubs off on the volunteers at Centurion, who
devote much of their time and energy to reviewing trial transcripts
and writing detailed reports. It's a long process, and the volunteers
learn as they go. Jim says that they know pretty early on if they're
cut out for this kind of work.*

Sometimes it's overwhelming for all of us. For example,
look at this huge stack of papers. This is one of the reports
I'm just getting to that a volunteer wrote in 1992.

There is no other organization in the country like Centurion. And yet I don't want to see the ministry become a
huge organization with branches all over. Right now the
current budget is around $420,000 a year, and I can't see
this as being any more than perhaps double that amount. If
it did, that would mean that I would become an adminis-
trator. And then there's the reality of raising money every
year—just because I think we can reach a financial goal
doesn't mean we will.

What Jim has given up to pursue his calling is balanced by the fulfillment of doing what he knows he was meant to do.

Sometimes I miss having a family. It's like a wave coming in and going back out. When it comes in, I yearn for the intimacy of being married and raising children. There are other times—just as often and maybe more—when the wave recedes and I don't feel that way anymore.

I'm rich in friendship and life's work, and I'm privileged to have this ministry. It fits my personality like a glove—solving mysteries and doing investigations, making something out of nothing, and bringing together a diverse group of people in one common enterprise.

I look back now and realize that my life was saved literally when I saved George "Chiefie" de Los Santos's life. If it weren't for him, I wouldn't be doing this work. He gave my life meaning.

Part Four

AFTER THE CALL

When we originally planned this section, we thought we'd interview retirees who could look back on their lives and tell us about the satisfaction of retirement after the call.

But, in truth, there is no such thing as "after" the call. The call keeps calling. And you will keep loving your work. How long will that be? That's entirely up to you.

Isn't that nice to know?

19

Please Yourself

*Each of us has different ways of
combining our senses and experiences. And this
gives us our own particular path to follow.*

STANLEY SELENGUT

67, Entrepreneur

Just do what you want. Simple as that.

You are hardwired to love your true life's work. And something deep down inside you will compel you forward. You will be drawn to your calling as soon as you allow yourself to know your heart's desire. And you will be amazed at how easy it is.

You will succeed beyond your wildest imaginings, because it stands to reason that when you live your life ac-

cording to the dictates of your own yearnings and lean-
ings, you will also be more attuned to the genuine needs of
the marketplace. And you will know how to motivate your
employees according to the dictates of their own heart's
desires.

It's understandable to doubt this. But all you need to do
is listen to the ones who have retired wealthy and happy.
They will tell you that they consistently chose toward
their joy.

*Now that they have put their Fifth Avenue town house on the mar-
ket, Stanley Selengut and his wife, Irma, live in their five-bedroom
beachside villa in Bridgehampton. But actually finding them there is
rare. They are more likely to be in Australia or Belize or New
Guinea or Yosemite or Hong Kong. They have racked up so many
frequent-flier miles over the decades they can now fly the world first
class on coach fare. Pretty much forever.*

*Stanley says he is retired, but in truth governments all over the
world are seeking out his advice on how they can cash in on the
booming tourism industry, all the while preserving their indigenous
culture and precious natural ecosystems. And he continues to collect
prestigious awards and recognition—the most recent being the 1997*

Environmental Award presented by Smithsonian *magazine and the American Society of Travel Agents.*

Stanley has done what he has wanted his entire life. And now he presents to the world the example and the technical expertise to prove that it is possible to live according to your principles, protect the planet, and profit immensely in the effort. All at the same time.

All this might not have happened if Stanley had not been dismissed from his first job after college. His offense: telling his supervisor that he wanted to contribute more to his job.

In one way it came as a relief, but in another he was once again faced with the question of how to earn a living—a question that held a constant theme throughout his youth.

I was born in 1929, when people were really poor. My father had a little linoleum business. In those days the trolley car was a nickel. But he would carry the roll of linoleum on his shoulder and his bucket of paste in his other hand and walk twenty blocks to his customer's home instead of spending the nickel. I grew up with a sense of hardship deeply imprinted in my mind.

During those years I developed a minor learning and memory problem. The educational systems in those days depended on memorization, and I remember being accused of not trying because I did very poorly in school.

So I had to figure out circuitous ways of remembering

things. For instance, Columbus discovered America in 1492. I would think, well, I was living at 3214 Loring Place and I went to P.S. 92. The first two numbers of my address added up to five and the first two numbers of 1492 added up to five. And P.S. 92 finished the year Columbus landed.

See? I had to learn how to understand things in a different way rather than simply remember them. Being forced to figure out new paths around the problem was probably the beginning of my development as a creative problem solver.

If you don't do well in school as a kid you get a real inferiority complex built up and you lose your self-confidence. Even though they say Einstein was dyslexic, I didn't really believe it. It takes a long time to get a feeling for yourself and who you are and that you really are competent.

Hating school as he did, he forged his father's signature at seventeen and joined the marines. Sent to China for two years, he received his first taste of exotic cultures, and completed a high school equivalency course. But his education had just begun. His formal education would end with college, but his journey of self-discovery would lead to a life of world adventures.

After the service I bummed around as an itinerant carpenter for a while and finally came to the conclusion that I really needed an education. I graduated with a civil engineering degree, primarily to please my father. But I discovered that it's not a creative field at all. The architects get to do all the imaginative stuff, and the civil engineer simply figures out how to get it built. But it's a good discipline because it teaches you how to build. And you don't waste time with things that are impractical.

I went out on my first big project—connecting the New Jersey Turnpike and the Holland Tunnel. I was stationed on this rig where a machine kept banging on this piling. It was my job to count how many blows it took to bang the thing down an inch. Most times I would count up to ten; in rocky places I would get as high as thirteen. Here I had worked really hard for two years getting my degree and I'm stuck with this dumb-dumb nothing job.

When the supervisor came around, I said, "Look, I really think I'm qualified for more than this kind of work." And he said, "That was what you were hired to do." I told him I was unhappy doing it. And he fired me then and there.

I got fired from my first job and never worked for anybody else again.

Thanks to the booming economy, Stanley was soon working again as a construction superintendent at a housing development, with an unusual compensation agreement—his first stake in his future, which would then forever be about the marriage of technology, economics, and the native creativity of people the world over.

Instead of paying me a decent salary, the builder paid

me a very low salary and a percentage of the profits. The development sold out, and my share of the profits was about $20,000. Which was terrific!

About the same time I read an article in the *New York Times* about how they finished a section of the Pan American Highway through Mexico to Guatemala. Now you could drive all the way from Alaska to Costa Rica, then ship your car across the Pacific Ocean and drive the rest of the way to Chile.

My first wife, Leona, and I put big truck springs on our 1957 Chevy, took out the backseat and filled the space with spare tires and gas cans, and put a box on the top for camping gear. And we headed south.

It was really a wonderful trip. We were just amazed at the wonderful crafts we saw and the skills of the mountain people—ceramics and especially the beautiful hats and ponchos and other woven goods. Leona decided to open a store back in New York selling these crafts. And with one phone call to her best friend, Rita Grossblatt, they agreed to open a shop in Greenwich Village and we would start buying what we found during the rest of the trip and shipping it up north.

By the time we got back, it was in the fall, and we had tons of stuff that we had shipped back. The girls thought the face masks and ponchos would be good for skiing. So they set up a window display, which a buyer from Saks saw and asked if the girls would sell wholesale.

One day a *Life* photographer took a picture of a couple of kids flying over some moguls with our ponchos flying in the wind. We made a two-page spread in *Life*, which also ran our address and prices. And the mailman was dropping off sacks of mail every day with orders, complete with checks, totaling up to more than 10,000 face masks alone.

The girls were frantic and wanted to get out of the business. Rita's husband, who was an accountant and hated accounting, suggested we take over the business instead, and I soon found myself in Peru to get those face masks made.

And this was the first time I really felt that I was coming into my own finally.

While in Peru, Stanley came to meet and understand further the indigenous people. Stanley's own disadvantaged background helped him both sympathize and respect that wasted genius of this race which had been forced out of Lima and herded to the mountains by the Spanish conquistadores. It was truly through this respect that he discovered ways to help them achieve a more comfortable life, all the while motivating them to produce mass numbers of knitted and woven goods.

But these were the days before ecological and cultural sensitivity was commonplace, and Stanley learned an extremely valuable lesson in the consequences of upsetting delicate balances that had evolved over generations.

These people were very self-sufficient and didn't have a money economy. If they needed something they couldn't make themselves, they would just make a mask so they could sell it and buy exactly what they needed. And no more.

My first thought was to pay them more, but that turned out to be counterproductive. They could get what they wanted quicker and then work less. And if you were at all cross with them or seemed pushy, they would just completely withdraw.

Eventually I found out that the unpleasant, time-consuming part of the work was in clipping the sheep, carding the wool, spinning the yarn, dyeing it, and so on. The knitting was the easiest part and the most pleasant. And for them the real treat was working with store-bought wool. This was really special to them. The yarn was softer and easier to work with, and the dyes were bright and fast.

With store-bought wool, making the masks would be fun, and they could sit and talk and nurse their children and do all kinds of things while they made these masks. So I just bought tons of bright-colored yarn from Lima and was giving out skeins all over the place. Before you knew it, masks were pouring in.

For the first time in my life I felt really needed. As they made more money they were able to buy better produce from the coast, so they became healthier, and they kept warm with kerosene lamps, which they were able to buy with money. Soon we ended up with twenty-two villages working for us, with over two thousand employees.

But after several years the fashion and demand for Peruvian crafts dried up. And here Stanley's company had created a new economy with no way to keep it supplied all by itself. This was a heavy responsibility, which he met by using those old tricks he had learned as a schoolboy to figure out new ways of solving problems. And his old skills brought him to a place where he learned his next lesson—the value of recruiting powerful contacts. For the very first time he would match government and corporate interests to protect and preserve not his only business interests but the precious legacy of native cultures and crafts.

About this time President Kennedy had established his Alliance for Progress to help raise the living standards for people in Latin America. Since I knew the communities that worked for us needed more customers than just us, I went to Washington and started banging on doors. I told my story over and over again, how there were all these people who were trained and eager to work.

Around 6:00 P.M. that day I finally landed in the office of the chief of cooperative development for Latin America. I explained to Robert Bonham that Sears had seventy stores in Latin America and if they could manufacture some of their product there as well, they could pump the profits back into the economy, so the people there could then afford to buy more from Sears again.

To get rid of me more than anything else, he said, "If you can get Sears interested, I'm interested." So I ran to the nearest pay phone, called Sears, and told the story all over again.

The next thing I knew, the government sent me with Sears executive Mary Lewis all over Latin America looking for products that Sears could manufacture there. We came up with three thousand products, and Sears opened its first import shop.

There are times when you're ready to do things, and what has happened to you in the past prepares you for your next stage in life. I sold my half of the import business to the Grossblatts and went to work for the Kennedy Administration's Office of Economic Opportunity, developing business opportunities for the American Indians, the elderly, and the people who live in the Appalachians. It was really an exciting time, running around the country convincing the local governments that they should promote marketing cooperatives when they really didn't give a hoot about the well-being of their people in the first place.

That was such rewarding work, proving over and over

again that you can effect change to benefit whole disadvantaged populations and make money too.

But Stanley's own income plummeted during that time. He had been earning well into the six figures with his import business, but the maximum fee he could charge as a consultant to the U.S. government was only $100 a day. And he was spending $44 every day commuting from his New York home to his Washington office. But he had invested his import earnings well—in his civil engineering training and building experience. With the leftover income every year, Stanley would buy a lot and build, or he would buy an old house and renovate.

I was able to go from a position of being purely money-oriented to enjoying working for the government for its own sake, because I had already accumulated enough wealth so that the wealth itself was generating its own income.

Each year I would buy a lot or two on Fire Island and build a couple of rentals, making each house nicer than its neighbors. When New York went into a funk, I was able to buy mansions and convert them not into a lot of small apartments but into a few really elegant apartments. This wasn't work; it was really easy.

Everything I've done has been a combination of my past being applied to what I'm doing now.

Over the decades, Stanley's work continued to build on itself, combining lessons of the past with an increasingly vivid vision of both the future's growing potential and rapidly depleting resources. Consequently, with his growing real estate holdings and entrepreneurial ventures based on preserving the environment and indigenous cultures, Stanley has made a career of playing a sort of ecological Monopoly.

Chance meetings over the years and new technological developments with construction materials made from recycled products, combined with an ever-increasing appreciation of the delicacy of indigenous cultures, have made him a world-recognized expert in creating a tourism industry that sustains and preserves the many lands and ways of civilizations throughout the world.

As a result of a little freebie consulting to help the Rockefeller-renovated South Bronx tenements and return the apartments to their original residents, I was introduced to the owners of some beautiful real estate on St. John. And that's how I started Maho Bay and began exploring new methods of sustainable development.

I discovered in my early days at Maho Bay there was a real demand for a beautiful, low-cost vacation destination that encourages people to interact with nature and learn more about their environment and the way they impact on it.

While a lot of developers throughout the world were

bulldozing fragile ecosystems and paving over the very thing that was attracting tourists, I was developing new, low-impact construction methods. The elevated board-walks preserved the foliage that kept the topsoil from slid-ing into the bay, for instance. And then we discovered we could suspend the electricity and plumbing under the walkways so landscape isn't marred by visible utilities.

We've been able to use solar showers, photovoltaics, and other environmentally instructive technology that demon-strates to our guests exactly how they impact the resources where they live. And all of this can be achieved without sacrificing our guests' comfort. Some of our units are sold out so far in advance that even I can't get into them.

This project is my chance to use everything I have learned, to create something where there are no losers: the customer benefits, my staff benefits, I benefit, and the com-munity at large benefits.

I'm an entrepreneur first of all. For me the masterpiece of entrepreneurship is the model that works for everybody, where there are no losers and where everything is in a bal-ance and working together for everyone's benefit and prof-itability.

He was once a man who knocked on doors, but the world is now coming to him. Vacation destinations throughout the world are invit-

ing Stanley to further develop his concepts of sustainable develop-
ment and demonstrate how this new way of life can attract tourism.

In my earlier days I never had the confidence that what
I was doing was like cream, that it would rise to the top of
the milk no matter what happened. But now what I'm doing is like cream. Sustainable development is inevitably the
way of the future. As populous countries become more affluent, they're going to want better things in life. But we
have to learn to live within our environmental means to
survive as a species.

The levels I'm moving in now are amazing. I have a lease
agreement with a large beachfront property in Oahu, and
we're negotiating for properties in Baja, California; Ber-
muda; and throughout the U.S. park system. And I'm just
about to fly to Scotland to accept an award from the
Smithsonian. It's really awesome to be elevated to this
league when all I was doing was just making a living. Following your heart can lead you to spectacular heights. You
can never tell where you'll end up.

Maybe it's the perspective of age: As you get older you
develop a dexterity in your craft that makes it more plea-
surable. You may not have the same passions as you do
when you're younger, but you develop a pleasure in your
ability to use the things you've learned all your life.

Each of us has different ways of combining our senses

and experiences. And this gives us our own particular path to follow. A lot of subtleties will come into play as you gather knowledge and develop your ability to understand other people's points of view and your ability to deal with situations.

The important thing is finding your own path. Intellectually you might disagree with that path, and you might wish you were someone else. But if this is the way you function best, this is the way you function best. The more you fight it, the less you will achieve in your life.

And, Stanley says, following your calling does not mean abandoning the wish for a life of material wealth and comfort.

I would never do anything that isn't profitable. Money is very important to me. It's my sustainability.

Developing a successful business requires identifying a need that must be met. And in this time when there are so many changes, there will be more needs that will crop up as we adjust to those changes.

There's a new future out there. See it as an opportunity to make money. But make that money by performing a service that will fill a need.

20

Pass On the Power

*We often try to see ourselves in other
people. What is more important is to have
other people see us in themselves.*

JACK MORTON

86, Founder, the Jack Morton Company

Growing older doesn't automatically earn you a badge of wisdom, unless you've put in the effort—every day of your life—to follow your heart's desire and make the most of whatever challenges come your way. That means you share your good fortune with others and shoulder the bad times with dignity.

For it's these lifelong experiences, both the highs and the lows, that bring clarity of insight and a unique opportunity for a new calling—to guide those younger than you to open their eyes to a future full of possibilities.

Octogenarian Jack Morton has spent his life pursuing multiple callings, from working in theaters in his youth and booking entertainment to focusing his energies on being a good husband and father to building a multimedia empire, now run by his son.

With several offices around the country, the Jack Morton Company produces business and entertainment programs for meetings and conventions. At Jack's office, the walls display autographed photos of many of the entertainers he has worked with over the years—George Burns, Jack Benny, Shirley Jones, Bob Hope, Red Skelton.

Semiretired now, Jack still lectures at George Washington University on the art of selling and writes essays on his philosophy of work and life. He often speaks in aphorisms: "The best travelers always have a map." "Egos should never be seen or heard." "Learning is not a part-time job." "Religion without morality is a contradiction."

He's titled his latest collection of essays If You Can't Sing, Hum.

The idea actually came from my wife, Anne. We were in church one Sunday and she was urging me to sing and not just hold the hymnal. I don't sing well, and whistling was out. Then she turned to me and said, "If you can't sing, hum."

I got to thinking about her suggestion and how it applies to more than just singing in church. For example, we can't all be in first place in our work, so often we play second fiddle. But that shouldn't be discouraging. The second instrumentalists are essential to any orchestra because they complement those in the first chairs.

In education, there are assistant professors, assistant principals, and assistant teachers, without whose skills there would be a complete breakdown of the total effort. In sports, the pitcher or quarterback may be the main attraction, but it's all the other players on the team who make the game hum!

The point is, we do what we must and can do, and each of us plays a role along with others for our mutual success.

I have no idea how many lives I've touched or affected, especially through our company. I can't count all the people who have impacted my life over the years. People who claim to be self-made are ignoring the influence of others. Everyone needs help along the way. In truth, none of us could have gotten where we are without building on foundations laid by others.

Growing up in the early 1900s, Jack lived in a simpler time when hard work was not only valued, it was necessary for survival. It was also a time when people knew their neighbors and reached out to help one another.

I was born in 1910, when the country was the country. You might live in a town, but it was a country town. All the sophistication was in New York and Chicago—mostly gangster-related!

Everyone was taught to work, but I had a lot of people helping me along the way. I learned early on that I couldn't do anything worth a damn by myself. My mother died when I was six, and that broke up the family. My father ran a farm and couldn't handle all of us.

My younger sister was adopted by an aunt, and the twins went to live with relatives. My older brothers went to work on their own. But I was in between—too old to be adopted, too young to be out on my own. So I boarded with other families. Once my father remarried a few years later, I went home to live with him.

I learned how to get along with people, and they always gave me good advice. People saw qualities in me that, with some help, could make me a better person. It wasn't charity. It was compassion for a fellow human being, a compassion I don't see much of today.

When my children say they feel sad because I lost my mother at a young age, I tell them, "Yes, but I had more than one mother." I know there are surrogate parents out there today who do a better job of parenting than the genuine article.

Today, so many kids are in trouble because they don't have the parental support or backing of genuine friends. They're self-absorbed—wrapped up in their own problems—and don't see that the friends they rely on are having the same problems!

And they won't go to older people who can help them. A child without the guidance of older people is lost. You can't learn anything from people who don't know any more than you do!

Jack was fortunate as a young boy that the adults around him looked out for him and gave him good advice. He learned from them the lessons of caring and compassion.

One of my brothers was an apprentice to an optometrist but would never be able to become one himself because he didn't have a high school diploma. The importance of finishing high school was no insight on my part; it was the realization by my brothers that what had handicapped them, they weren't about to let happen to me.

Another brother got me an after-school job with a jeweler and watchmaker. I'd go in and sweep the place for about fifty cents a week. Once I complained to my boss about having to clean the spittoon, and he took me aside, looked me in the eye, and said, "Any honest labor is honorable."

I worked at a jewelry store where the owner's son had a terrible reputation—he stole from his father and ran around with women. One day at the store the owner reached into the drawer for a gun and tried to shoot himself in the heart—right in front of me—but the bullet hit his pocket watch and went around his side.

To my young eyes this was the true meaning of being in real trouble. Since I was on my own much of the time, I could've gotten into real trouble myself, but everyone watched out for me. Even the owner's son made sure I stayed out of trouble! I think I had a whole flock of guardian angels surrounding me.

In between school and work, Jack spent his days and nights with his first love: music. It is a passion that has endured throughout the many decades of his life, providing him with a livelihood he could not have imagined as a youngster.

Music has always been a part of my life. It started with my mother singing hymns and playing the concertina. Music can create a mood, and I think it's one of the most wonderful forms of communication in the world.

When I was twelve, I worked at a silent-movie theater,

and one of my jobs was to change the roll of music on the player piano. I'd stand in the back and watch the movie and think, Wouldn't it be great to have the music match the action? Every Saturday the manager wanted me to play Schubert's *Serenade* to accompany the western; that's not the right music to go with galloping horses!

The irony is that my success in the entertainment industry has been due to my failure to be a musician! I tried taking piano lessons, and I was terrible. But I did know what was good to listen to and good to dance to. And that's how I came to be successful booking orchestras for local dances.

By the time I finished college, I had put together a dozen orchestras. One day I went to a client who said he had just met with one of my competitors. The competitor asked him why he would book an orchestra from me, a nonmusician. I said, "Well, you're paying for it. What do you know about music?" He replied, "All I know is what is good to listen to and easy to dance to." And I said, "That's all I know too!"

Jack may have been playing second fiddle to the musicians, but he was the one who knew how to orchestrate a perfect performance. His business did so well that he started producing shows for conventions and booking top entertainers. To save money and have more control of the show, he served as the master of ceremonies for most of his productions.

I was not the typical MC. I introduced the acts instead of telling jokes and getting carried away with telling stories about myself, like most MCs do. One of my shows was ruined when I let a famous personality be the MC. He kept talking about himself. But when it came time to introduce the lead act, he had to reach in his pocket—I can still see it to this day—and pull out a piece of paper to read the name of the headliner!

Since I was taught to be honest growing up, that's how I built my business. I also wanted my business to be clean, and that became my reputation: "If you work with Jack Morton, you'll have a clean show."

I knew what was profane, what was base. Sure, everyone had a secret and personal curiosity about such things, but if you wanted that, you went to the burlesque shows. And even then, there was none of the obscene display you see today on TV and in the movies.

I think people are becoming fed up with TV shows and films exhibiting all the sexual behavior, immorality, crime, destitution, and destruction imaginable. Meanwhile, it's no wonder our children are old and experienced beyond their years by the time they're thirteen or fourteen.

Jack holds the industry responsible for the lack of values found in much of today's entertainment. And he's disgusted with what he says are the industry's lame attempts to lay the blame elsewhere.

The entertainment industry has money galore and will continue to use it to promote its own position. For example, an industry spokesman asserted that parents, not television, were to blame for their children's problems because they could not control them. All I have to say is any child-proof device you put on a television—if your child can't deactivate it, then you've raised an idiot!

Greed and a disregard of human values are what drive the entertainment industry. Perhaps we can find some hope in Goethe, the poet and philosopher, who said, "Those whom the gods would destroy, they first make blind with greed."

After a highly successful career of owning his company, Jack is content to let his son build upon that dream. Now he has turned his attention to putting a lifetime of thoughts on paper. He says he's not sure why he feels compelled to do it, except that he still has something to say and more to share with the world.

Many people don't realize that life is a process. When we make mistakes, we should then try to correct them. We must learn to make adjustments. But still some people are never satisfied. They want to run instead of walk. They want to graduate when they're still in eighth grade.

I've had my share of sinking spells. But I never felt sorry for myself. I never had a problem that I couldn't eventually cope with by making adjustments. Our company went broke a few years ago, and we had to borrow and mortgage just to get back on our feet. People who don't adjust to the hard times, who just bail out—they don't understand that it's the hard times and problems that build character. Intelligent people learn more from their mistakes than from their successes.

Jack has found from a lifetime of personal and professional experience that the following suggestions—what he calls commandments—are good guidelines to live by.

Associate with older, more experienced people. Look to others for help and advice; don't try to go it alone. Put those you admire in your mind as to what you'd like to be like. Make your goals human instead of material. Have a sense of humor and be able to laugh at yourself—there is no subject so serious that it can't be helped by a little humor. Lose yourself in helping others.

We often try to see ourselves in other people. What is more important is to have other people see us in themselves.

Afterword

Listen for Your Calling

Several years ago the two of us—still uncertain of our own callings—took a screenwriting class together. Or at least started to. That was one of many classes we have registered for together over the years. We would end up abandoning them partway through because we were getting more out of our own conversations. Once we even ditched the entire annual conference of the American Society of Journalists and Authors because we found ourselves brainstorming the outline of our first book idea over take-out cheeseburgers in our expensive New York City hotel room. That book never happened, but it was a good exercise to prepare us for brainstorming this book. We just didn't know it at the time.

Back to the screenwriting class. By the second or third session, the class was studying the script for the 1985 film *Witness*, starring Kelly McGillis and Harrison Ford. There was agreement all around: *Witness* is a detective story. We stared at each other in astonishment. No, it isn't! *Witness* is a love story!

A love story? Or a detective story? It's like a poem: it all depends on what you find in it.

Listening for your calling is also both a detective story and a love story. Your life might have been filled with clues, with red herrings, with misleading seductions, with disappointments. It's your task to sort all that out to arrive at the conclusion that will crack your case.

And that conclusion will bring you love. Love for the way you spend your days. Love for yourself. Love for the people you work with.

There is no one right way to find your calling. Your path is your own. For that reason we didn't lay out a firm how-to program. We hope that *Find Your Calling, Love Your Life* is for you like a poem, the meaning you need rising from its pages through the voices of the people we interviewed.

For us, writing the book has been a shared calling—the calling of a friendship of sixteen years. When we met at the start of our writing careers at a nonprofit organization we worked for, it seemed as though the universe began laughing. And so did we . . . to the point where one of us had to quit before we both got fired.

But there was no getting around it, there was a creative chemistry between us that told us our friendship was meant for something important. And for many years we tried this and that, marketing our talents as freelance writers packaged under a single word, Finney&Dasch. But no project, no assignment, no dream, seemed to be quite as good as what our chemistry seemed to call for.

We even laughed during the terrible, moneyless recession years of the early 1990s. There was laughter in our friendship, but there was no joy in our work. In fact, we hated it.

But that darned chemistry was still there. Worries and struggles that would rip any friendship apart couldn't touch ours. We still laughed.

We knew we had two things going for us: our friendship and our talents. There was something important that we had to do. *But what was it?*

What were we supposed to do with this friendship and talent, when we had lost the faith that there was joy in work?

Eventually we turned that question into a prayer. And the answer came, like a piano crashing through the ceiling. Suddenly. Big and noisy: Our job was to write the story of how work *does* bring joy.

And the book was born. Just like that. *Find Your Calling, Love Your Life* became both a detective story and a love story. Our job was to search out people who had found a way to fully express themselves and their life's purpose through their work. And our job *description* included all the things we do and love best: travel and spend a year talking with profoundly happy people.

And we had fun! After so many years of waking up in the cold, acrid sweat of anxiety; of delivering take-out dinners for that extra margin of vital pocket change; of wondering where the next check would come from; of wondering if we'd ever enjoy writing again, we were suddenly having a blast! Research for this book took us to George Lucas's Skywalker Ranch for lunch; down the Pacific Coast highway in a convertible; to hot and dusty Phoenix, where we stared at dead scorpions in a basement lab; to a Bridgehampton villa, where we ate dinner by candlelight just one dune away from the crashing Atlantic surf; to Bonaire, where one of us celebrated a milestone birthday by watching the sun rise over a turquoise sea.

We have loved our calling.

You, too, are meant to love your calling. But you may have to do a little detective work first. And that's okay. In retrospect you'll see that the search is worth it. In fact, the search is part of the preparation process.

And how will you know you've found your calling? There will be joy. And there will be laughter.

About the Authors

Martha Finney has been speaking and writing about work in America for over ten years. She lives and works on a beautiful creek near Annapolis, Maryland.

Deborah Dasch lives in Baltimore, Maryland, where she pursues multiple callings—writer, editor, fledgling producer, and aspiring novelist.

To contact the authors, or for more information on workshops and speaking engagements, write to

OurCalling@aol.com
or
OurCalling
P.O. Box 2189
Annapolis, MD 21404-2189